GOD, SEX, DRUGS
& OTHER THINGS

God, Sex, Drugs

&

Other Things

Howard Frankl

Foreword by Ernesto Cardenal

NewSouth Books

Montgomery

NewSouth Books
105 S. Court Street
Montgomery, AL 36104

Publisher's Cataloging-in-Publication data

Frankl, Howard
God, sex, drugs & other things / Howard Frankl ;
with a foreword by Ernesto Cardenal.
p. cm.

ISBN 978-1-60306-383-8 (paperback)
ISBN 978-1-60306-384-5 (ebook)

I. Title.

2016939588

Design by Randall Williams
Printed in the United States of America

TO

INOUE HIROTA

B. G.

ELIZABETH GREER

THREE PERSONS IN ONE

Contents

Foreword

ERNESTO CARDENAL

(TRANSLATED BY ROGER BUNCH)

I have known Howard Frankl for more than fifty years. I studied in a Trappist monastery in the United States, and later was in the Benedictine monastery in Cuernavaca, Mexico, studying to become a priest, when he arrived asking me for baptismal instruction because he wanted to become a Catholic. He'd just had a transformative moment in his life. While smoking marijuana and reading an article in *Time* magazine about the expanding universe, he had a clear, inner experience of God (which he relates in this book), and this was the reason he came to me asking for baptismal instruction.

To teach an adult what they need to believe to be Catholic isn't easy, and I'd never done it—in fact, I've never done it again. There are things in our faith that are difficult to believe even for those of us who have always believed them (and for others they aren't just hard to believe, but impossible), but Howard had no difficulty with the dogma. As I explained the beliefs using a thick catechism book for adults from the monastery's library, they seemed like obvious truths to him, and he was excited to know them. I remember he rebelled just one time, when the catechism said that Saint Thomas Aquinas claimed that a pure atheist doesn't exist; that no matter how atheistic you are, deep inside you have to have some idea of God. But Howard said that contradicted his experience: that though he was from a Jewish family, he'd grown up without any faith in God until God was revealed to him when he smoked marijuana. I told him that this disagreement wouldn't be an obstacle to baptism; that the catechism claimed Saint Thomas Aquinas said this, but I didn't know how he said it; and besides it wasn't dogma. In the end, I was his baptismal godfather in the beautiful colonial church in the small Mexican town of Santa María de Ahuacatitlán. The baptism of Howard Frankl filled him with joy.

My godson wanted to be a monk in the Benedictine monastery, but God, through the events of his life, helped him realize that wasn't his vocation, that he was called to marry and be a therapist. Though in a way, he's been a monk this whole time.

Howard Frankl also has another vocation. He hadn't written before, but soon he was a fresh and original writer, with a book that is hard to categorize. A book that bookstores and libraries won't know where to shelve. In fact, it has a title that can be surprising: *God, Sex, Drugs & Other Things*. The "other things" are the two chapters "Money" and "Murder," in addition to other topics throughout the book. I find God present not just in the chapter by that name, but also in the chapters on drugs, sex, money, and even murder. I'd advise the bookseller and librarian to put the book in the Religion section, but also in other sections, including Psychotherapy, Politics, Current Events, Americana, etc.

Or maybe this isn't another vocation of Howard Frankl's. Maybe the God that was revealed to him when he smoked marijuana and read *Time* magazine, which led him to baptism, also called him to be a writer, and inspired the book the reader holds.

The appearance of God is described in this book in this way:

> . . . I lost all sense of time, all sense of space other than its infinite vastness; there was no light, and nothing to see, just pure experience of the presence of God. For those of you who have not had such an experience, I can best describe it by calling it indescribable . . .

This book on God, sex, drugs, and other things is a bold book, and in it are things writers don't dare say. Only God. And he has said them in the Bible. But since we read the Bible so often, those things don't shock us. They shock us when someone says the same things in a new way. This is an orthodox book, but to some it will not seem so, because it presents the dogmas with a freshness and originality we're not used to.

The believer (nor the unbeliever) shouldn't find it strange if it says in this book that everything we say about God is false. That's the most definite thing we can say about God, and traditional Christian theology has said it since ancient times. This way of talking about God even has a Greek name. And it is because the reality of God (even his existence) is beyond our understanding, to the point where to say he exists is false.

What is not false is that we can unite with him (or her) about whom our understanding is false. This book describes a type of prayer for union called Contemplative Prayer, and it is rare to find a clearer, more exact description of this hard-to-describe prayer. This isn't a prayer we attain through skill, nor voluntarily, but is a gift we receive, a prayer we can only practice if we receive that gift; but there are many who receive it, sometimes without knowing, believing that when they experience that state it isn't prayer. It is the prayer that those who have received this gift should practice, and one sign that you have the gift is that other types of prayer are unpleasant for you, even impossible.

THIS BOOK, ON RELIGION and other themes, isn't just about ideas. It's eminently autobiographical, which makes it a pleasure. Who isn't interested when someone tells us about his or her life? Howard shares frankly his intimate relationships, and those of people he's known, some of whom have been saints. And since he's a therapist, the anecdotes from his professional practice are engaging.

There are also many poetic passages. I find what he says about the vagina at the beginning of the chapter titled "Sex" to be especially poetic. And later in the same chapter, the reader will find the Nativity described with an audacity I don't think anyone has ever had: the Mystery of the Incarnation between urine and shit. This may seem sacrilege or blasphemy, but it's the way the Son of God was born, and the way the author saw his own son born. Tertullian, the theologian of the early church, was right when, as he said, he was stunned that God would emerge from shameful parts and feed himself in a ridiculous way. The same thing is said here, but in a more crude way. It's dogma, and you don't mess with dogma, or you shouldn't. It's the Renaissance art and Christmas cards that show a different Nativity, the one that should be considered sacrilege and blasphemy.

As for something both Catholics and Protestants do—portraying Jesus and Mary as non-Jews—the least we can call that is a perverse heresy.

Something else I admire in this book is the author's profound knowledge of drugs—those he's tried and those he's studied. And we can't ask for a more reliable and objective way to judge theory and practice than this.

Of all the legal and illegal drugs, the only addiction the author suffered from was that for tobacco, which he started using when he was seventeen. That was in the day, as he remembers it, when Camel cigarettes were advertised as the one preferred by doctors, who were shown in lab coats recommending them. (Which I remember too, and Camel was my choice when I was a student in New York.) What the author says of this addiction is horrifying.

Many people, almost everyone, will be surprised by the revelation in this book on a substance called tryptophan. It's found in foods like chicken and hamburger because it's a component of protein, though the Japanese have made it into a white powder. It's the transformation of a nutrient, as was done in the remote past with bread: flour was converted into something new, but that didn't mean it was no longer a food. This marvelous white powder that the Japanese isolated, which can be taken orally or intravenously, was prohibited by the FDA, and for years you could only get it by prescription, as if it were a drug. It's as though, in the remote past, they had prohibited bread.

Money is seldom called an addiction, and it's the most pernicious of all. This book helps us see, among many other things, that money caused the pollution of Los Angeles. Or that it took from the people of Los Angeles their streetcars.

This book runs against the current because it is the book of a prophet. When it speaks of crimes, it speaks of the war crimes of the United States. No other people on earth exercise the self-criticism of North Americans. And though in other countries we're very critical of the United States government, we also recognize this great virtue of the North American people, a virtue found in this book.

The point of the book is the salvation of all humanity (and all the rest of the cosmic creation).

Acknowledgments

My wife, Bernice Teresa: Muse, best friend. Most valued nation. Richest natural resource.

Ernesto Cardenal, without whom this book could never have been written.

John Fantham, old friend, forgiven and forgiving.

Dennis Marc, old friend, forgiving and forgiven.

Alan Hoffer, friend of more than sixty-five years, an inspiration.

Max Parker, brother, who in his youth picked tons of cotton, sometimes more than two hundred fifty pounds in a day, and was paid little for it.

Mark Schack, son and counselor.

Thom Zajac, editor extraordinaire.

George McClendon, inspirer, friend of forty years, brother, mentor, explorer, pioneer.

Joyce Breiman, flower.

Chayim Barton, gentle protector.

Daniel Reid, friend of fifty years, destroyer, creator.

Horace Randall Williams, friend, brother, ultimate editor.

Finally, Robert Emmet Kelly, friend of fifty years, and mentor, who often said, "Man is nothing, if not contradictory."

GOD, SEX, DRUGS
& OTHER THINGS

1

Drugs

Jesus took drugs on the cross; legal ones of course, because the Roman police offered them to him to deal with his pain and discomfort, and after he took them he could function more adequately and went on to finish a climactic part in the history of humanity. Vinegary wine is what they offered him, a legal drug of choice for death penalty sufferers of that time.

That was in one Gospel version. But in another Gospel version of his life, they offer him the same drug at the same time, and he doesn't take it. And still goes on to become a success, depending on your point of view.

I wonder how the fundamentalists deal with these seemingly contradictory parts of the Bible. Did Jesus use legal drugs or didn't he? I mean if the Bible is just literally true, then for sure he did use drugs, at least that one time. But on the other hand, if the Bible is literally true, then he didn't use them that one time.

I used legal drugs once for sure, no two versions about it. I was applying for a place in a university's graduate school of social work, because I wanted to be a psychotherapist. This social work school, which had an excellent reputation, was running a research project on the best criteria for admission, so one year it would admit on the basis of past work experience, and then the next year it would admit on the basis of the oral interview, and so on. The idea was to go back some day and see which year produced the best social workers. Then they'd know the best criterion for selecting new social work students in the future.

The year I applied they were using undergraduate grades as the sole criterion for selection, and they told us so. No sweat for me. Duck soup. I had graduated with honors from UCLA, had been elected Phi Beta Kappa, had all A's and one B in my major subject. I sent off my application with a copy of my sure-ticket sure-fire transcripts.

They also had us applicants write a one-page biographical statement, which they assured us was only a formality, and for the most part it was. But in my case it wasn't. My biography started with the statement, "I want to be a social worker to serve God," and then went on to talk about God and Jesus, serving my brother, and so on. I knew there was a bit of risk in this, but because my grades were exceptionally high, and grades were the norm by which selection was decided, I was confident of being accepted.

A friend of mine whose grades were considerably lower than mine got a letter of acceptance. Time passed. No letter for me. A week or two later my letter came: I hadn't been accepted. No explanation, just that all the elect had been notified; I wasn't one of the elect, but, if I wanted, I could be on the school's alternate list.

Ahhhh . . . that biographical statement. Those words about God. I stuffed my sense of injustice out of sight and phoned the school and talked to the head of admissions, Dr. Olander. We set a time for an appointment to talk things over.

Before our interview, wrought with anger, fear, and confusion, I took a drug, a wine-and-vinegar-type drug because it was legal in the sense that a doctor had prescribed it and a big drug company had profited from making and then hyping it, but sort of illegal in the sense that a friend of mine whose doctor had prescribed it for her gave it to me, and so I showed up to the fateful interview under the influence of a controlled substance; which is to say, drugged.

I was therefore numb to my feelings of fear, anger, and injustice (did Jesus have any of these feelings on the cross?). Instead, I was feeling somewhat stuporous, compliant, and lacking in any kind of passion (Jesus is said to have felt passion).

Stuporous, compliant, and lacking in any kind of passion seems to have been just the sort of person the school was looking for, and a day or two after our one-hour meeting I was informed I'd been accepted into the program. They had found me to be less crazy than they feared when reading my biographical statement, but then my insanity had been masked by one capsule of Valium when they met me.

Actually, I had taken enough illegal drugs in the years prior to the vinegar-and-wine Valium capsule to have affected my psyche immeasurably. Five years before my admissions interview I had smoked my first marijuana cigarette, against my better judgment and morality, but to please a wonderful and lustrous woman who, to my surprise, pulled a doobie out of her brassiere and, wearing an intoxicating smile, held it before me. At the time, I was a hard-core addict of nicotine, a then-legal and rather lauded drug, so smoking the joint was no problem at all. I knew all about holding smoke deep in the pit of my lungs.

Once we had burned the marijuana down to a small charred nub I began to rail and grump at my lovely companion, telling her that the inhalation was having no effect whatsoever on me, until I noticed my right hand, which had suddenly taken on a magic quality that made watching it imperative. The hand traveled back and forth in front of my eyes, did arabesques and Balinese dancing moves. It changed hues and, to some extent, shapes. My hand had become altogether lovely and enchanting, and was perhaps not my hand at all, but more likely the hand of hands, or the wand of wands, or the frond of fronds.

When the spell ended, and I don't know how long it lasted, I came back to my usual way of seeing, and realized there was more to this marijuana thing than I'd been led to believe. And then I began laughing. And laughing and laughing: deep-in-the-gut and -heart laughter, the kind that loosens the soul. I was laughing at myself, and my old prejudiced J. Edgar Hoover-indoctrinated views on marijuana. I was in my early twenties, this was 1957, and I hadn't yet learned to laugh much about myself deeply those days; somehow, without thinking about it, I knew marijuana was going to be good for me, and that I'd be with it for a long, long time.

A couple of months later and I was holding down my first real job, teaching at an all-white middle-class high school, and smoking marijuana evenings and weekends. The day job helped me learn my subject matter, which was writing and literature, and the evening and weekend marijuana smoking taught me how to relax, how to love love-making more, how to listen to music better, and how to see the glory in flowers. To be honest, I couldn't have done the work of high school teaching so well without the avocation of pot smoking.

Then the obligatory military draft that was currently in place took me away for a couple of years, and I went to a government technical school at Fort Ord, California, where I was taught various practical occupational skills, like how to run a bayonet into my foreign brothers and shout "Kill!" at the same time. I also learned to shoot phosphorous grenades from the end of my M-1 rifle, grenades that would burn the flesh off the bones of anyone within twenty yards of their detonation. There were many other new skills taught here, like moving silently in the dark the better to kill you. Our tax dollars at work.

When I returned to high school teaching my control of classroom discipline had improved, but I felt more disaffected from my country. By the end of the school term I had saved enough money to live a year abroad, and I left my job with excellent references and a bon voyage. I had been smoking marijuana the whole time—in the army, and then through the school year. My feelings were hurt when the student newspaper wrote a very unfavorable and inaccurate article about pot smoking. It had a quote from our government's then drug czar, Joseph Anslinger, which read, "The marijuana user is a vicious moral leper who should be punished swiftly and without impunity." I hadn't robbed any gas stations or gone on to heroin, and I'd done a good job as a soldier and schoolteacher. So I reeled with the harshness of the government expert's declaration, and its reminder that I'd be put in prison for two years if the wrong people knew.

This was 1959, and only a number of blacks and beatniks were enjoying marijuana.

DRUGS CAN DO YOU good, you know. Helped Jesus on the cross. Or didn't, depending on which version of the Gospel you read. Drugs helped me a lot during my year abroad, starting out in Mexico City, and I loved Mexico so much I stayed there for thirteen months and then went back to my country, homesick for fresh milk and a better grade of beefsteak. Besides, once I learned Spanish I realized that as an alien I was often being made fun of, when riding a bus, for example, by people I hadn't had the pleasure of being introduced to.

I had picked Mexico for my first stop because I'd heard marijuana was plentiful there and easy to get. I also knew there was a brisk trade in prostitution.

Within three months I discovered a need for working that surfaced once I had lived week after week without it, and I took a position as English instructor at a private school for the children of the city's wealthy.

I also collected varieties of marijuana like an English gentleman might collect varieties of fine tea, and I stashed them in glass bottles, smoked them whole or blended, and many an evening traveled far away from my normal mind.

I also visited prostitutes during those days, but this was not really to my liking, and so I established an exclusive relationship with one such hard-working young woman that was both unprofessional and fun for the two of us. We went to parties together, the zoo, I visited her home and family and, in short, we became rather traditional lovers. Her name was Maria. Our relationship was for the most part unremarkable, although it eventually occasioned my need for a long series of urethral antibiotic suppositories upon my return to a more medically advanced society.

But while still in Mexico an indeed remarkable thing happened. One evening while alone on my bed and reading a *Time* magazine article on the latest theories of the expanding universe, to my complete amazement and surprise I found God. Or, more accurately, God found me.

I had been an atheist since the age of four when my babysitter, after I asked her if there was a God, told me I'd have to decide that one for myself, and I myself decided to believe from that time forward that there was no God, and that no God had ever existed. I had had only one lapse of faith, and that at the age of five when my kitten got its furry gray head caught in a knothole in our garage wall and I found myself praying that our handyman would saw through the entrapping board in time to keep the soft, wide-eyed puff from breaking its scrawny neck during the frenzied panic its ensnarement had triggered.

Other than that I had remained relatively firm in my conviction that there was no God and thought myself adept at enjoying the out-arguing of anyone who held to the contrary, Catholic priests and Catholic friends especially, because their faith seemed especially illogical, and besides, their eyes were mild, even in the face of my petulant reasonings.

God chose to pay me a first visit that evening when I was loaded with dope and alone on a bed in Mexico reading the article in the Science section of *Time*. Why just then I don't know, but there it was: I lost all sense of time, all sense of space other than its infinite vastness, there was no light, and nothing to see, just pure experience of the presence of God. For those of you who have not had such an experience I can best describe it by calling it indescribable. If all your life you'd been blind and then suddenly saw . . . it was another sense, but a sense like no other. It was not ideas about God, or the recent footsteps of God, it was God as embrace, God as all. One God. True God.

And then I was back in the room, permanently changed. A friend dropped by. I cried in his arms. And then I cried some more.

THIS EXPERIENCE LASTED ALL of a week and by then the doubts were setting in fast. After ten days a growing wall of doubt was beginning to hide the meaning of the memory, especially the doubt that said it was just the marijuana (though God knows I and others had smoked marijuana often enough with no such experience). At the two-week mark when I had walls all around my belief and was starting to nail the roof down, and when I'd had many an evening to get thoroughly doped up without any sort of visit from anyone or anything, God struck again, again while I'm on the bed in the room and loaded on marijuana; this time my eyes are wide open, I can see, only instead of God being nowhere and nothing like the first time, God is now everywhere.

God is infusing the ashtray with indescribable divine presence, and the ashes, and the cigarette butts; God is shining up through the cheap linoleum floor; God is flowing up from the boarding house bedspread; God is pouring out of my arms and hands; God is flooding in through the walls, and radiating out of the window shades; God is lighting and enlivening the air in the room. And after the message is thoroughly delivered, it is over, and I'm left in the room laughing with delight, wonder, and awesome, exuberant joy.

This time I cannot begin to get over my new faith, which is, after all, a gift, not even after two or three weeks have gone by, and I do something that might at first seem strange: I prepare to apply for entrance into the Catholic church.

Let me briefly explain.

As a senior in college I'd become bored with studies, and though I kept my grades up, I began a not-for-credit exploration into comparative religion and read about as many of the so-called major religions as I could, and as deeply. I concluded that if I ever did believe in God I'd become a Catholic, the religion that seemed to me to be the most inclusive and therefore the one that had the most to offer.

I was baptized June 10, 1961. I was twenty-seven years old at the time.

Caution: Potential side effect of marijuana smoking is turning into a Catholic, but so infrequently we don't even bother putting it on the label.

I HAVE ALSO USED cocaine, LSD, mescaline, peyote, and psilocybin, but not that much. And a few prescribed drugs, but not that much. By not that much I mean less than ten times each, except for cocaine, which would be less than a hundred times.

The first time I took LSD, the drug was legal. That was in May of 1965, and the newspapers and news magazines had been debating for a year or two whether to criminalize it. My brother had tried it and told me all it did for him was to make music sound better. A dear friend had taken it several times and had gone through very powerful and positively transforming experiences, or so he said, and he, like my brother, would be commonly considered an upstanding member of middle-class society.

Around this time the media had gone on one of their inimical smear campaigns, where truth is shut out in the cold while propaganda in the guise of reportage works its hypnotic magic on the population. *Time* during this period ran a regular feature called "Trip of the Week," a framed box of boldfaced type thumbnailing some citizen's recent experience on LSD; for example:

> Thomas Rathbone, age 33, of Semicity, Florida, took LSD at home and believed he had turned into an orange. After three weeks, he still thinks he's an orange.

Just honest objective reporting, but the feature shouldn't have been called "Trip of the Week"; it should have been called "Bad Trip of the Week." They simply didn't publish the good ones.

All the prior reports of good results from LSD, the healing experiences for many alcoholics, the comforting experiences for many of the dying, the religious experiences of groups of clergy that tried it, were soon forgotten under the mantra of negative journalism, and when the government stepped in, there was little opposition anywhere.

They canceled the research funds like the federal grant that paid for a psychologist named Stanley Groff who worked at the National Institute of Mental Health in Maryland, or the ones at UCLA. As is so often the case with powerful people, opinion is the goal, not truth. They set a date in May when taking LSD would be illegal, and a few days before that day came I swallowed the prescribed amount.

My friend Harold Oaklander was there at my home as my babysitter and guide. He was the man who had already taken LSD several times and enjoyed the experiences.

I needed someone there because I was so afraid.

I had somehow gotten it firmly in mind that I was going to die during this first acid trip.

After ingestion, nothing for a few minutes, then the onset of drug effects that soon became so overwhelming that I had to lie down on the floor and close my eyes. Darkness poured in from all the corners and I soon discovered myself in a very vast black space with a small bit of light far above. I flew up toward the light like a diver rising from the depths to distant air and sunlight.

As I sped closer the light suddenly transformed into a giant arch of multi-colored glass, much like the vault and glass of some great Gothic cathedral;

but as quickly as I arrived I shot through the luminescent multicolors and continued rising until there was absolutely *nothing* else there but God, not even me. Which is to say, as there was nothing but God, I discovered I was God. I was the ground of being; before me was nothing; other than me was a contradiction in terms. And like Adam in the Langston Hughes poem, I was lonely. I really didn't like it there. I was surprised to be there. I hadn't thought of this possibility: that I would take LSD and consequently discover I was God, Alpha, and there was none else but me nor ever had been. How I got out of that rather desperate condition of awareness, with some eternal twistings and spiralings and turnings, I'll never quite know, let alone describe, but I ended up alone on the living room floor, with Harold Oaklander doing dishes in the kitchen nearby, and I could not walk and I could not crawl, and I bawled like a baby: loud, all-out, gushing tears, raging and longing for Harold's attention and care.

Instead of dying I'd been born.

And by the way, while I was writing this I was drinking a cup of fine Darjeeling tea, also a drug, but a legal one at this time.

THERE WERE OTHER EXPERIENCES during my first trip on LSD: one in which time almost stood still and twenty seconds felt exactly like three or four hours; one in which Harold's face and body broke down and gradually turned into mine (and mine turned into his); one in which I died a French officer on a green battlefield, my face mushed into the grass and one booted foot caught in my horse's stirrup; and a personal favorite, my last seconds as a dying gopher down in a dirt tunnel with the prongs of a Macabee Gopher Trap spearing my furry chest and shoulders.

About eight hours after the first swallow I began to slowly dismount from the wild ride that lysergic acid had given me, but the aftereffects lingered. My then wife, who had been frightened off by the brouhaha that the press had made, returned, and Harold departed. I assured her that all was well now, and got into the bathtub for a warm soak. But all wasn't quite well. I had very large gaps in my memory (I didn't remember that we were in the process of leaving our rented home for one we were buying, rather a major event at the time), and I generally felt "spaced-out," as the saying of those days went, rather as if my head had been soundly kicked by a friendly mule and then doubled in size and filled with oatmeal.

The next day arrived with a prolonged and pronounced inner haze. I wasn't much good for anything but staring vacantly into a distance. And after all, there was a lot to think about, including where did my Catholic religion go during the short while I was God, or for that matter, throughout the whole mystery tour?

Two days after the trip I returned to my job at Orange County Mental Health Clinic. I put on my white cotton blazer with the badge that had my name and "Psychiatric Social Worker" printed on it, and went to the Monday morning staff meeting that always began our work week. It was held in the director's office, with its windowless yellow walls, institutional desk and chairs, and total lack of decor. The public professionalism of its day.

There we sat: the social workers in their waist-length white starched jackets, and the psychiatrists and psychologists in their knee-length white starched coats, each of us with a rectangular name badge pinned over his right breast pocket. It was 1966 and we all wore neckties, except Charlie Galbo, a psychologist. Charlie wore a bow tie.

The director-psychiatrist sat behind his gray metal desk at the top end of the rectangular room; his chair was nearest the door. The rest of us sat in two long rows with the backs of our chairs against opposing walls. We were facing each other. I was in the throes of coming down from LSD, still way out there, and no longer inhabiting what I formerly called a sense of sanity.

As the opening business of the week was transacted, the announcements, the hellos and banter, the polite disagreements and ponderings that came with thinking about the county's crazy people we'd been tax-funded to serve, I found myself writhing and sweating inside my proper and sane exterior. After all, I had been God only two days ago, to say nothing of a gopher and a dying French cavalry officer. My memory was still faulty, things looked drabber than ever in this bunker of an office, and I was having a firsthand Kafkaesque moment.

In short, I was out of my mind, if my mind was defined as the one I'd left with on Friday afternoon, and the very key question arose, a decision, really, as to whether I wanted to return to what used to pass for reality. It took only a few minutes—I had a good job, a wife, a child on the way, and a house in escrow: it was worth it. I descended from the fuzzy heights and re-entered mental health as defined by Orange County California psychiatrists in the mid-1960s.

My normal chores at the mental health clinic included evaluating people to see if they needed to go into the locked ward for crazies. Only once do I remember someone who had been thrown into a disabling tizzy after finishing their date with a spot of LSD, and that's only once in three years at a time when lots of folks were trying the drug. The young man in question had a history of emotional deprivation and injury that in time probably would have landed him in the loony bin whether he took drugs or not. Unlike me, he had little to lose by giving up what we usually call sanity. It was time for him to try something new, and the poor wretch didn't know about the chamber of horrors we called Inpatient Ward. For him it probably seemed a good gamble.

Another chore that fell to many members of our staff was delivering talks to groups in the community, like the friends and relatives of the patients we were drugging and electroshocking into dull submission on a daily basis. This kind of public information function was state-mandated, and though we might not have thought it at the time, we were agents of the state.

A psychiatrist named Dan Castille gave all of our talks on LSD. He was our in-house expert and in much demand during these days when the drug was still a hot and controversial topic. Dan was older and gentlemanly, had the bearing and smoothness of a congressional politician, and was in fact an all-around good man.

But the day came when Dan couldn't make the speaking engagement he'd agreed to, a meeting before the entire congregation of a church, and asked me to fill in for him. He told me the outlines of what he'd been saying about LSD all around Orange County, and believe me it was uniformly bad, and based on my own experience with LSD a lot of it was just plain misleading falsehood.

So I asked Dan, whom I very much liked, if he'd ever taken LSD, and

Dan said, no, he hadn't. So I asked him why, and he said that he thought that would spoil his objectivity.

Being new to the call of church speaking, and not wanting to disclose the firsthand-experience source of my disagreement with Dan, I spoke no further with him on the topic.

But I prepared to bring truth to the pilgrims soon to assemble in the house of God, and I worked up a sweat preparing my talk, making sure I covered both sides of the issue: what was good about the drug, and who it was good for; and what was bad about the drug, and why some folks should stay away from it, just like a very fat man should avoid trying to complete a marathon in under ten minutes a mile.

The evening came. I arrived at the large white wooden church's door, and I was wearing my white shirt, jacket, and tie, and I was just a bit short of breath and sweaty, and I was prepared. Three or four elders, dressed like me, but older, taller, and heavier, met me at the entrance with cordiality somewhat laced by tension, and told me the outlines of the talk they wanted to hear me give.

Like Dan's talk, theirs boiled down to *Time* magazine's "Trip of the Week," in which a man is still thinking he's an orange three weeks after his first LSD experience. They kept me at the back of the hall for about five minutes, going over the outlines of what they wanted said, and took my muteness for agreement. Then we marched up to the altar, turned around, and one of the men introduced me.

I talked to the congregation for about an hour, and I included the story of the man who thought he was an orange, and a lot of other stories like it, but then I covered the other side of reality, the one in which LSD had done a lot of people a lot of good, and I talked about how the media was smearing LSD with a lying one-sided account, and that how the stuff affected you was a lot more about you than it, and how I thought the government's response of criminalizing it was a serious mistake.

The congregation seemed polite and interested enough, but the moment I finished the men who had met me at the church door stood up in the back of the room and began talking loud and rapidly. They gave the man who believed he was an orange speech all over again. They gave the same speech they had told me to give. Then they called the meeting to a halt without leaving time for questions and I was out the door.

Somehow Dan Castille and I never talked about this event in much detail. And I was never asked to play guest expert on LSD again. Unlike Dan, I had actually taken LSD, so unlike Dan I was no longer objective.

I WENT ON ABOUT ten more LSD trips after that; then I had a bad trip and never took it again, nor do I need or wish to.

The statute of limitations has long passed on all my drug use, and now I can only be arrested if some authority plants a drug on me for that purpose. So perhaps in a way I've committed the perfect crime, but not one that hurt anyone, like killing or cheating, crimes you'd have to confess and repent of as a Catholic.

I confessed my drug use to priests on occasion, and one said he wasn't sure it was a sin at all, and thought it probably wasn't, and another said it just wasn't a sin, period. No one asked for as much as a Hail Mary.

However, when I confessed being out-of-control angry at my children the priests took note, and gave both counsel and penance.

I took illegal drugs from age twenty-three to somewhere past sixty. During this period of almost forty years I finished graduate school, held steady work, married and raised children, all the while listening to the largely lying and inaccurate picture the public was being fed, and fearful of speaking my truth because the truth would land me in jail quickly enough, and along the way take my state licenses and diplomates as a psychotherapist.

I'm not sure why we're being lied to about drugs, or so many other things, for that matter, though I know there's a lot of money tied up in those lies, most recently the millions of dollars made by those bastards running the growing international corporation prison industry.

A FINAL STORY: For ten years my office shared a waiting room with the office of a psychologist friend. One of his clients was an ex-nun, a lovely lady who was having some trouble adjusting to life outside the cloister. Gradually the lady and I established a friendly relationship, all during the minutes she spent in our waiting room before her session began, and she invited me to visit the parochial school classroom in which she taught third-graders.

The hour I arrived had coincidentally been set aside for drug education, part of an ongoing program designed by the county office of education. The boys and girls, mostly eight- and nine-year-olds, sat pleasantly at their desks, the girls in Catholic school green plaid pinafore dresses, the boys in green corduroy pants and white shirts. They were at ease and enjoying themselves. They obviously loved their lovable teacher.

The lesson went smoothly. The teacher went over material on marijuana, which they seemed to have been studying for at least a few days. The students enthusiastically raised their hands to answer her questions, and they had obviously done their homework and learned their lesson: if you smoked marijuana you would soon be dropping out of school, losing interest in life, feeling the joy drain out of your soul, and then you would go out and rob a gas station. After a few years at most you would take all the other kinds of drugs including LSD and turn into an orange.

I left the classroom shaken and some days later talked to my dear waiting room friend about my impressions. Of course she had been taking all the fearful propaganda and spreading it on faith: faith that the experts at County Office of Education would be planning a truthful curriculum.

Perhaps like Dan Castille those county people were maintaining their objectivity by never taking a drug.

I have long lost my virginal objectivity in that sense, so I simply state that illegal drugs are an awful lot like alcohol. They can kill you fast or slow, ruin your marriage, and take away your job. Or they can add years and pleasure to your life, or in some cases help you with your thirst for God. Don't put us in jail again for a dry martini. And stop putting us in jail for a burnt doobie.

EVERY CHRISTIAN SHOULD KNOW that each person's life has its crosses. But the Christian cross, by Biblical definition, is light and easy; at least for many of us who came to Jesus for relief from unbearable labor and heavy burdens.

And most everyone, Christian and non-Christian alike, takes a drug now and then to make their personal cross more bearable at a particular time (*See:* Jesus, wine and vinegar). But it's hellish when use turns into addiction.

Experts define addiction in two ways:

First, you're an addict if you can't control how often you take the drug you love and hate, or how much of it. And/or, you're an addict when: Your drug of choice spoils your intimate social life; especially if it fucks up your marriage badly, or screws you up as a mommy or daddy. Or if it messes with your time at work, like drunkenly dropping wrenches in moving gears, or calling in sick on too many Mondays.

I counseled a while in an alcohol rehab program. All the clients, and there were hundreds of them, had two tickets for drunk driving in a single year. These folks had to choose between taking this program or doing jail time and paying a fine.

When I started, the program director had me do thirty days of abstinence from alcohol and drugs, which was also what every client had to start with. He had me monitored in weekly sessions with the clinical director, who was a friend of mine and a proven expert in substance abuse.

I had two lapses during the thirty days, having one or two drinks per lapse, and duly confessed to my buddy. My performance constituted a passing grade. I was not an alcoholic by clinical definition, although I wasn't a star performer either.

And sure enough, many of the men in my caseload couldn't go three days without a drink, and some of them couldn't go one day; and so by professional definition they were out-of-control addicts, alcoholics, and drunks. And all of them eventually owned the problems that booze had brought to their homes and work sites, so again they had met the definition.

I saw these jaspers both in individual and group counseling sessions. And all of them were addicts by professional definition.

The problem was they didn't meet another criterion the experts rarely mention: they didn't think they were alcoholics, addicts or drunks. And so they weren't going to want to do much about what we outsiders called an addiction, and what the drunks called a run of bad luck with the Highway Patrol. They were going to pass their time in therapy having fun, and not dealing with a serious problem they consciously didn't know existed.

Freud called this kind of not-seeing-the-obvious, Denial. Denial is when you won't say yes to the obvious, because you find the obvious too painful a condition to face.

Drunks go into denial in a charming and often humorous way. In group counseling, when I sat with twenty or more of these comedians, there was usually a lot of laughter and fun and sociability, and there was no serious talking about drinking as a problem.

My job was to get them to face reality; that is, reality as we professionals defined it.

When the defense of denial is attacked by what we call Reason, the response is usually anger. This is why most people won't attack a drunk's denial system (ask any drunk's husband or wife what I mean). And this is partly why the denial system can live for so many years, sometimes a lifetime.

BUT AT THIS POINT I'm going to quit talking about the legal drug alcohol for a while, and talk about another legal drug, nicotine. Nicotine is usually found in cigarettes. I want to talk about nicotine for a while because cigarettes are my only drug addiction.

And because I am an addict, I know firsthand what addiction really is. I know it not from some outside perspective, like the professionals who talk about self-control or interference in work or family. I know it from the perspective of one who has found himself coughing and hacking and hurting and frightened of dying and stinking and gasping and still going out at three in the morning in below-freezing weather because there were no cigarettes in the apartment.

Harmful Addiction means none at all, or way too much.

I had my first cigarette around age sixteen and was addicted without knowing it by seventeen. Those were the days when Camel cigarettes were advertised as the brand most preferred by doctors. No one knew how deadly cigarettes were.

Humphrey Bogart did it with tough sophistication. William Powell did it with savoir-faire. All the cool men did it. I got the Bogart mannerisms down to a T. I liked the hit of smoke when it bounced off the bottom of my fully inflated lungs. And now science tells me I liked the way my mind raced a little faster when the nicotine started shaking my brain cells.

I smoked as much as I could, and that was called chain-smoking, light-
ing the new cigarette with the burning stub of the cigarette I was finishing.
At this rate I could smoke three packs a day of non-filtered cigarettes, and
I did just that for years.

When my cigarette cough got too deep and loud, and my lungs hurt
too much to keep the pace up, I switched to two packs a day, and when I
could no longer keep that pace up I went to filtered cigarettes.

I wanted to stop and I found I couldn't. I was an addict. I smoked as many
cigarettes a day as I could; only the amount of pain and coughing limited
me. There was enough information out on cigarettes and cancer for me to
know I was killing myself. I was entirely out of denial. But I couldn't stop.

During these frightening days I read a long biography of Sigmund Freud,
the famous fellow who chain-smoked cigars. The biographer was a friend
and colleague of Freud's and his words were too uncritically admiring to
really involve me. After the text of the book ends there's an appendix made
up of the clinical notes on Freud's eventually fatal course of mouth cancer,
cancer brought on by his habitual and probably addictive nonstop cigar
smoking. Freud's physician carefully documents the prolonged suffering
and periodic surgeries that Freud underwent as his mouth and jaws were
gradually cut away from the rest of his body. There's also the part at the end
when the consummately stoic Freud meekly and feebly requests an overdose
of morphine just to end what had become an altogether unbearable life.

It was these cold medical notes, not the warm and admiring prose of
the friendly biographer, that grabbed my heart and pulled hard on it. When
I had finished reading them, I put the book down on my desk and burst
out in tears, crying for poor stoic old Sigmund Freud, and all the ungodly
misery he had been through, and just how much misery it had taken to
tame his proud spirit.

When my eyes cleared I looked to the left of my desk at the chair which
the client usually took. There sat Dr. Freud in all his conservative Viennese
finery.

Our visit was a short one. I was sure of my visitor's identity, and felt that
my earnest compassion for his suffering had somehow earned me the honor of
his dropping in. He asked me what I wanted (he was in his all-therapist mode).

"I want to stop smoking cigarettes," I said.

Dr. Freud pointed to my shirt pocket; a recently opened pack of cigarettes nestled inside it.

"Stop smoking," he said in a firm voice of complete authority.

I reached into my shirt pocket, took out the cigarette pack, and dropped it into the metal trash can.

I was done smoking. And when I looked up, Freud was gone.

The cure was effective, and lasted three or four years until I played the saboteur. Its oddest feature was the complete absence of any urge to smoke. In all my past attempts, lasting anywhere from less than a day to just under two weeks, the urge to smoke was strong and incessant. After my visit with Freud, abstinence was easy, even when having coffee during heated conversation with a friend who was smoking, and that had very often been the hurdle that even my best efforts tripped over.

I saw this miraculous cure that occurred after twenty years of addictive smoking as a great conversation piece, but I was wrong. People noticed I had stopped smoking and wondered how, but my story was not to their general liking. And after all, when one is a therapist, one does not always want to be thought of as crazy. So little by little I held the blessed event secret, and gradually began taking personal credit for having quit the deadly addiction.

When I had all but forgotten my visit from Saint Sigmund, patron saint of smokers, and replaced the actual memory with a smug delusion about personal strength and willpower, I smoked another cigarette.

Just one, I thought. No problem. I was no longer addicted, I thought. I've got this thing under control, I thought.

And man, did I enjoy that smoke. My first in years. The flavor. The faint bang the smoke made on the bottom of my lungs. Even the wooziness that the virgin nicotine inhaler gets. No sweat.

Just one.

Then about two weeks later: Just another one.

It took me less than three months to regain full addiction. Hacking, hurting, burning, smelling. Right back to the advanced stages of cigarette slavery, and cigarettes are mean and tormenting, murderous little masters, especially when they've been cutting away at your insides little by little for more than two decades.

So, again, the sense of helplessness that a real addiction brings: Can't stop. Want to stop. Can't stop. Must stop. Can't stop.

None or too much.

And then, after a long while, *Help me God.*

After two or three more years of compulsive self-poisoning I was unable to smoke more than half a pack a day, and that was with filtered, mentholated tobacco, a far cry from my preferred unfiltered straight tobacco Humphrey Bogart first loves. My body was letting me know that I was killing myself, but I couldn't stop doing my pathetic daily maximum lethal dose.

And I did talk to God a lot those days. A lot. I remembered Saint Sigmund's visit. I repented of having forgotten the source of my deliverance. I promised God if he took me off the hook a second time I would always give him all the credit. And eventually he did. And I do.

On November 10, 1976, I was sitting in a diner having coffee with a friend and smoking a cigarette; we both were. There was a sudden pain in my throat, like many other pains I'd been having for years, but more severe, and I put the cigarette down, and I haven't had a cigarette since.

Just like with the earlier Freudian miracle, all compulsion had vanished; there wasn't even so much as a strong urge to smoke. There was no losing battle to torment me. There was no battle at all. Just Divine deliverance, and a peaceful feeling around the issue of cigarettes. Thank you, Jesus.

So that is my one firsthand experience with harmful addiction. And as a cigarette addict I know harmful addiction is: None or too much. That I can never have one more cigarette, any more than an alcoholic can have one more drink, or a cocaine addict one more snort.

OH YES, AND I may already have killed myself with cigarettes. The doctors tell me I have what they call Fifty Pack Years; that's because I smoked three packs, two packs, and finally one pack a day for about twenty-five years, and it averages out to two packs a day, or Fifty Pack Years.

I heard about this when a specialist removed a small tumor from the roof of my mouth a few years ago. That I have a lifetime vulnerability to all the illnesses heavy smokers are heir to, even though I've been abstinent for more than thirty years, and ran my first marathon more than fifteen years ago.

Two of my good friends died of alcoholism some years after they quit drinking. Same deal. Harmful addiction.

HAVE YOU HEARD ABOUT halo effect, when we see something or someone as either all good or all bad?

We see no bad at all if we're looking at someone or something through our Positive Halo Effect. And we see no good at all if we're looking at something or someone through our Negative Halo Effect.

Teenagers idolizing certain entertainers, or churchgoers idolizing their pastors, that's Positive Halo Effect. The hatred a Muslim feels for a pork chop, or a KKK member feels for a black person or a Jew, that's Negative Halo Effect.

Sometimes halo effects are downright pleasurable and harmless, and sometimes they are tools of the Devil. Having your first crush, or even your second or third, that can be Positive Halo Effect at its harmless finest.

Political leaders and some church leaders are expert at turning on our halo effects. Then we will work like a crazed person to get elected someone we know is going to break every promise they ever made, or we will yawn sleepily when we hear that our soldiers bulldozed sand over hundreds of young men ("enemy soldiers") and left them to smother and die.

Putting people in jail for just using cocaine and thinking that jailing them makes perfect sense, that's Negative Halo Effect, just the way the Devil likes us to have it.

I could have been put in prison countless times for my use of marijuana, cocaine, LSD, and other illegal drugs if I'd been caught by the authorities. I had no giant problem with any of these drugs, because I wasn't harmfully addicted in any sense of the word. As a matter of fact, throughout my drug use I have a record of good citizenship: as a cannery worker, carpenter, college student, teacher, social worker, soldier, health food marketer, and psychotherapist.

Plus, I did pretty well as a husband during the drug use days, and though one long-troubled marriage went under after sixteen years, the current one is still sacramentally blissful after thirty years, and in neither marriage was my drug use a source of complaint or difficulty. Honest.

Also my six sons are all up and running. The youngest is forty-three and the oldest is fifty-eight. None of them smoke cigarettes, thank God. None use illegal drugs.

But if justice had been executed, justice as it is currently and falsely conceived, I would have spent all those years in prison, subject to constant cruelty, torment, the threat of death and rape, removed from the possibility of contributing to society.

In God we trust? Give me a break, White Man.

There are also Positive Addictions, things we want to do, feel we have to do, and if we don't do them then we go into withdrawal and feel irritable and even depressed. But they are positive addictions because they add to our life rather than detract from it. Some people are addicted to aerobic exercise. Some to practicing the piano. This is usually O.K. And none of the Positive Addictions are drug addictions like, say, being addicted to coffee, so you don't get headaches and other flu-like symptoms if you stop doing them.

Medical feel-good drugs are legal, but you can't get them on the street like cigarettes and alcohol, which are also legal feel-good drugs. You have to get them from a pusher called a medical doctor, or M.D. The pusher is usually rich and fronts for the Big Legal Drug Companies, who are even richer, and who by the way have for sale some of the most toxic and harmful drugs in the universe.

The Big Legal Drug Companies also have the money to buy off the government and the media (they are among the few top-paying media advertisers, and their owners play golf and dine with the same president and senators who don't really want to know you).

And they have the money to hypnotize the general public with costly and expensive advertising and marketing, telling us lies and omitting truths in the sweetest fashion, just like Chevron Oil suggesting they are personally responsible for saving all the snow-capped mountains, all the deer and fawns, and an as-yet uncounted number of American eagles.

So I want to tell you a true and mysterious story about a series of current and expensive medical feel-good drugs. The story begins with something that isn't a drug at all. It's a health food. And I was in on this story because I worked for some years as a national sales manager in the Health Food Industry.

It's the story of tryptophan.

Tryptophan isn't classified as a drug by the U.S. government. They classify it as a food, same as chicken and hamburger.

Up to the middle of this century you could only find tryptophan in beans, corn, and other foods that had protein in them. Tryptophan never appeared alone. It was always hooked up to other parts of protein.

Then the Japanese found a way of isolating tryptophan, and they started selling it by the barrel. It looked like sugar or salt—just as white, but finer, more on the powdery side—and it didn't taste bad, either.

They sold it along with around twenty-five other powders, all of them other parts of what protein is made of; the Japanese had found a way of taking protein apart.

Doctors around the world bought up these barrels of food in multimillion dollar batches, because most of the powders would easily dissolve in water, so they could use them in intravenous feedings.

The old style of intravenous feeding was a water solution of sugar and salt. It kept you from dying of thirst, but after a few days your muscles started breaking down to feed you, because there wasn't any food to speak of in your IV bottle. With tryptophan and the other twenty-five or so parts of protein going into your veins, you stayed alive longer and stronger.

It was a great commercial market for the Japanese and a boon for the overall health of humanity.

Well, the Health Food Industry caught on to the idea that you could sell all these protein parts in capsules. The parts were called Free Form Amino Acids. Free Form Amino Acids because they could be put up in separate barrels; they didn't have to be all hooked together the way you found them in old-fashioned protein powders like whey or casein, which are both dry byproducts of milk.

It was a technological advance in food making, just like bread and wine were when they were first invented. I mean, taking wheat and doing all those things to it and adding all those things and then heating it into something new and wondrous like bread was a scientific breakthrough, miraculous, wildly inventive, but it happened so long ago we take it for granted. Or squeezing grapes and then knowing what to do with the juice so that it not only tastes real good but after a while it will get you happy or sad depending on your disposition; well, that was a heck of a technological advance in food making, but just because the scientists that did it wore homespun robes, turbans, and curly beards and lived a long time ago we tend to forget all about them and take wine for granted.

Some of these new Free Form Amino Acids had special effects, and tryptophan was one with very special effects.

In April 1983, Richard Wurtman, an M.I.T. professor and world-renowned expert on amino acids, published an article in *Scientific American* in which he said tryptophan will make a lot of us feel better, especially those of us who are depressed.

It will make us feel better because it's the nutritional raw material for something in our brain that makes us feel better. Something called serotonin.

And Richard Wurtman said tryptophan has no side effects. And it doesn't.

But not all that many people read *Scientific American*, so the discovery of tryptophan was rather slow and steady. I knew a number of people, some of them very smart and sensible people, who used tryptophan to help themselves with depression. And Synanon, a nationwide organization to help heroin addicts, had almost all its members taking tryptophan because it calmed them and helped them stay off hard drugs.

Since health food stores didn't have the mega-billion-dollar budgets of the big drug companies to advertise and market tryptophan, and since tryptophan was a food and not a drug, the popular discovery was taking its long sweet time.

But people were slowly learning about it anyway, and tryptophan was sure enough beginning to cut into the drug companies' profits, the profits they made on their own feel-good pills, like Librium and Valium, both prescribed drugs. You had to see and pay your doctor, your M.D., your Big Legal Drug Company pusher to get them.

So for a while there was a race on between a food, tryptophan, which was legal and made you feel good, and some drugs, like Librium and Valium which made you feel good, but the drugs were addictive and had side effects and tryptophan didn't. And the drugs were slowly losing their lead in this race.

But the drug companies weren't interested in selling tryptophan, because it was only a food and so they couldn't patent it and corner the market for it the way they do with their drugs.

But after a number of years, tryptophan finally did become famous and made the headlines and front pages. Only in a bad way. Because people were going into emergency rooms across the country sick as dogs, and a few were dying. And they had all just used tryptophan.

The FDA acted with unusual swiftness, and quickly and efficiently removed tryptophan from all the stores, and confiscated it from all the American distributors, who by now had lots of it stockpiled in their warehouses, because tryptophan sales had been rising so steadily.

The media kept reporting this drama as a top news story.

Meanwhile, the Health Food Industry, which was a small baby compared to the Goliath drug companies, protested vigorously, but to deaf FDA ears. They protested because tryptophan had been used for years without harm, and experts like Richard Wurtman had declared it safe and helpful.

The media didn't report the Health Food Industry objections.

Finally, you couldn't get tryptophan anymore without breaking the law. Kind of like marijuana. Then the media stopped talking about it altogether. Tryptophan had been sentenced to life imprisonment in a federal jail as a dangerous murderous substance. The story was done and yesterday's headlines.

And some months later two funny things happened.

The first funny thing was that a small story appeared on page C-7 or D-12 of the newspapers. C-7 and D-12 are the pages newspaper editors use when they don't care whether people notice what they are saying. Like they keep regurgitating their stories on Lady GaGa or Anthony Weiner on page one, but page C-7 or D-12 is for just once- or at most twice-printed stories, and then it's done and forget we mentioned it.

The small story I'm talking about said that a new discovery had been made about the tryptophan poisonings. It turned out that the tryptophan poisonings came from just one bad batch of tryptophan put out by one rather obscure Japanese manufacturer.

The poisonings were exactly like the poisonings that result from bad batches of chicken or hamburger shipped out of meat packinghouses. Tryptophan was no more dangerous than those other foods, chicken and hamburger, and far less fattening.

But the FDA never let tryptophan back into the market (although after a number of years they allowed another somewhat watered-down form of tryptophan in without saying why). The FDA kept tryptophan off the shelves and made no apologetic statements about their having given a good and harmless food the penalty of life imprisonment.

And the second funny thing that happened some months after the legal abduction and execution of the good food tryptophan was the much-heralded appearance of Prozac on the public stage. And then a growing chorus line of similar drugs, with show-drug names like Paxil and Zoloft.

Funny thing, but these fabulous show-drugs had something very much in common with the federally imprisoned humble new food, tryptophan: they were all about serotonin, the stuff that runs around our brains and makes us feel good.

Usually we get most of our serotonin from the tryptophan in food, any food that has a lot of protein in it, because, remember, serotonin is made from tryptophan, one of the ingredients of every protein.

That's why the pure tryptophan sold in health food stores was an upper for so many people. Tryptophan, as the internationally reputable scientist Richard Wurtman told the world in 1983, is the raw material, the nutritional precursor, of serotonin, and having lots of serotonin running around in our brains tends to make us feel better.

The show-drugs, on the other hand, are totally unnatural, which might be why they often start you out feeling like crap for a month or more, with headaches, constipation, sexual decline, and all the other signs that your body wants no part of them, though it gradually acclimates as well as it can, much in the way the slaves did after the initial shock of being kidnapped and robbed of their natural freedom: they put up with slavery, but they never felt good about it.

These new show-drugs, as you may remember from watching and listening to sincere-looking men in white coats with rectangular name tags over their right pocket, are, in the simple language of the drug company, "serotonin uptake inhibitors."

That means they take the serotonin you have, and rather than let it do what it was designed to do, they get it to recirculate in your brain again and again and again, and round and round and round, sort of like recirculating house water through your bathtub, dishwasher, toilet, and toothbrushing. They get the most out of the serotonin you have by "inhibiting its uptake."

And then you are no longer troubled by the things that used to trouble you: So your best friend died a few months ago. So you were defrauded by the government. So your common-law husband of ten years, the father of your two children, still refuses to legally marry you, or deed half of the house to you. It's O.K. You are a functioning member of society.

You are no longer fully alive and are chemically removed from feeling the full joy and sorrow, the actual agony and ecstasy of life, but you are a functioning member of society.

You can sit for forty hours a week and solder computer parts for decade after decade. And it's all O.K. Because you can no longer feel the pain that might indicate that there is something wrong with what's going on, and something wrong with the way you are relating to whatever that something is.

If only Prozac, Paxil, and Zoloft had come earlier. Rosa Parks would have gotten up and given her seat to a White Man on the bus. There might have been no march in Selma, Alabama. We would have been spared the turbulent emotions of what is being called Racial Integration. All the blacks who were pained by Jim Crow would be zombied out on Prozac. You know they were only troubled because they had bio-chemical imbalances. The trouble was genetic. Just like the bio-chemical imbalances of the folks who used to get pissed off after days and days soldering computer chips. Or the bio-chemical imbalances of the lady whose common-law husband wouldn't marry her. But they are all balanced now. They are no longer pained by their situation. They are all taking their serotonin uptake inhibitors. They are all on Prozac.

And the Big Legal Drug Companies and their pushers could have even further contributed to the robust economy. If they only had discovered serotonin-uptake inhibitors earlier.

Such brilliant scientists.

And by the way FDA, why did it take you so long to finally let the original tryptophan back on the market with hamburger and chicken?

And by the way Giant Media, why were there never headline stories about the mistake behind tryptophan's arrest? If ever conclusive evidence had emerged that O. J. Simpson didn't commit the crime we would have seen it day after day on page one. Tryptophan was jailed for at least three murders—that's one more than O. J., and tryptophan was later proven innocent. But there were no page one headlines pronouncing its innocence.

THE BIG LEGAL DRUG COMPANIES promote drugs the way Hollywood promotes stars, a sort of mass-hypnosis effort that leaves the public mouthing the slogans and platitudes it has been bombarded with for seemingly endless days or years. "Prozac corrects bio-chemical imbalance," whatever the hell that means. But it must be true, otherwise why would the handsome men in white coats with rectangular name badges over their hearts be telling me it is true?

And why would the network anchormen be telling me it is true, men (and sometimes women) who look like movie stars, and like movie stars are paid millions of dollars a year to talk in between the commercials made by million-dollar advertising agencies for billion-dollar industries.

"Dan, you're one of the front runners for news anchorman at CBS. We just have a few questions."

"Yes, sir."

"Well, first, Dan, what would you do if you heard something like, say, that the FDA was in cahoots with the biggest drug companies to get rid of one of their health food competitors?"

"Excuse me, do you mean our own FDA?"

"Yes, Dan, I do."

"Well, sir, that sounds like the sort of top story that really gets my juices going. I'd put all the resources at my disposal to get to the bottom of the rumor, and if there was real truth to it, I'd get it before the public, and keep it there until there was plenty of time for it to sink in."

"Yes, Dan, uhh ... thanks. We appreciate both your investigative reporter's enthusiasm and your candor. We'll get back to you after we've interviewed the other two candidates. But, remember, Dan, you're still a frontrunner."

THE DRUG XANAX IS not a star actor, just a character actor. It's been around for years, helps to add to the overall Big Legal Drug Company scene, but merely plods, rarely sparkles, in the economic drama.

Xanax has been prescribed for decades to thousands of people who come to the doctor-pusher each year because they're anxious, nervous or scared stiff. The doctor's right arm extends across the table. In his fist is a Xanax sample. Often the first one is free.

This is good business because Xanax is about as addictive as crack cocaine. And it doesn't do you one damn bit of good after two weeks, but by then you're addicted, so who cares.

Because you're addicted you get nervous and shaky when you try stopping it.

"Doctor, I got nervous and shaky when I tried getting off Xanax."

"Hmmmm. Sounds like you're not symptom-free yet. Maybe a biochemical imbalance. Better keep you on course a few months. Then, we'll have another look."

The doctor makes out because you can only get the stuff you're addicted to, and that he pushed you into, by coming to see him. Office visit. Fee. Office visit. Fee. Get it? And the drug company makes out because the do-nothing-but-addict-you drug has been a steady economic performer, just not a star, for decades.

Don't take my word for it. Read the article in the January 1993 issue of *Consumer Reports*.

Or better yet, read the Xanax section in the book *Toxic Psychiatry* by Peter Breggin, M.D. Dr. Breggin, a down-to-earth psychiatrist, a healer rather than a drug pusher, who also happens to be scholarly and a lover of truth, wrote a whole book in which the drug company and doctor-pusher myth of bio-chemical imbalance is carefully dismantled and then exposed as the flimsy money-making fraud it actually is.

Dr. Breggin used to work as a scholarly researcher for our government's National Institutes of Health. Then he got out and wrote a good book, a book I've never been able to get another doctor or psychiatrist to read.

Dr. Breggin points out that when the drug company submitted their successful plea for legalization of Xanax to the FDA, to make Xanax a legally prescribed feel-good drug, that there were only thirty-nine folks in the research sample. Thirty-nine people. Give me a break.

And that with those thirty-nine people, Xanax only outperformed the lowly placebo for the first two weeks. The last four weeks the placebo made people feel better than Xanax did.

And all this information was in the report the FDA reviewed. And based on this information the FDA certified Xanax as a legally prescribed feel-good drug.

And Xanax only makes you feel better for the two weeks it takes to addict you, and then you can pay for it doing nothing until you are ready for the rigors of withdrawal. But don't expect much help from the white-coated rich pusher that got you and a lot of other people hooked on it. You're helping to pay for his cabin in Lake Tahoe.

As ARISTOTLE AND OTHER smart guys pointed out, knowing what Feel Good is couldn't exist without knowing what Feel Bad is. We would never know ecstasy without having known agony.

Feel Good Drugs take you anywhere from a step or two to a long country mile on the road to feeling better, and sometimes they take you all the way to just feeling good beyond words.

And that's probably why school kids and old black jazz musicians still smoke dope, not that they always should, especially the little school kids; just that that's the usual reason behind it all—all this natural behavior that can land you in jail and that costs us taxpayers so damn much money and work to pay for governmental searching, destroying, and then ruthless and prolonged punishing.

I wish the so-called War on Drugs would cop to that. The National

Association for Justifying Cruelty talks like everyone is getting stoned and loaded just to be rebellious, or anti-social, or masochistic. No, they all start out doing it because they like feeling better, and sometimes just awfully, wonderfully good.

I speak from the personal experience of using and enjoying some currently illegal drugs alone in my home, or taking them and laughing or talking with friends, listening to music, dancing, having sex, and still having the time and energy to succeed in normal middle-class life, most probably better and with more joy than if that lovely lady had never pulled a joint out of her sweet brassiere.

And there are so many of us. But you won't find us quoted in the newspaper, not on the front page, and not on page D-7. You won't find us interviewed on the evening news, and we haven't been there since this massive wave, this ocean of lies started flowing into the minds of uninformed and gullible citizens. Citizens who, like Dan Castille, had never taken an illegal drug because they were afraid to lose their objectivity. Please, don't confuse us with real facts and real experience.

THE TRAGIC FACT IS that any Feel Good Drug can lead to harmful addiction. But that's the only fact that is being presented to us in the long and ponderous mass hypnosis of falsehood that tragically constitutes current consensual truth.

When I go to a restaurant that always features unlimited food in its long buffet line I often look around for the immensely obese people who gather to give in to their addictions, and they are always there, hunched over their high-piled plates and trying not be noticed, and the sight of them always helps me to eat a little less. I'm not a food addict.

There are also food addicts there who can't be spotted. These are the slender and often pretty ladies who are stuffing themselves compulsively, but who will later leave and puke it all up in a toilet bowl. We call them bulimics, the folks who binge and purge.

Food addiction of this sort, just like cocaine addiction, cigarette addiction, alcohol addiction, is very harmful to health, including psychological health, and is also harmful to both intimate and work relations.

If food weren't so necessary, the government and its cohort of professional punitive moralists could have all the folks who just like to have a piece of pecan pie now and then thrown into jail, with longer sentences for the restaurant owners.

Crimes like robbery, burglary, and murder don't hatch in a bottle, joint, or pile of white powder. Crimes gestate and are born in people, almost always in people who are psychologically unhealthy and unhappy. We are not getting them healthier and happier by putting them in prison for years, and our mistake costs us about $50,000 a year per person to keep them caught up in being further sickened and miserable by our laughably named "Correctional" system; $50,000 a year per person would buy a lot of therapy and education and social programming.

O.K., not everyone is fit for the streets, but for those folks who aren't, a less medievally cruel form of incarceration would do the whole cosmos good, and the average citizen might sleep a bit better, and need less Prozac to keep his social conscience numb.

Our prison populations are rising, our prison costs are rising, and most largely because of our lying attitude toward drugs. Drugs are not in and of themselves something to go to prison for. Don't put people in prison for smoking cigarettes or selling them. Don't put people in prison for drinking or selling alcohol. Don't put people in prison for using or selling marijuana, LSD, or cocaine. Lots of people do those things and live good lives. But almost all of them are too realistically frightened to let you know about it. If someone robs your house, let the law deal with it, whether or not the robber uses drugs. Drugs are not the problem, any more than the fistfights in bars are floating around in the beer bottles the guys drink out of.

Some of us drink beer and get happy. Some of us get amorous. Some of us get mean. The happy, the amorous, the mean—that's all in us, not in the beer. The things some drug users do, that's all in them, not in the white powder. Get them educated. Get them employed. Treat them as equals, as brothers. Educate them about drugs truthfully, not with fear tactics and lies. Watch them get better. Watch us all get better.

2

Sex

Father Aelred had been a solitary hermit for decades, then a monk and confessor at New Camaldoli Hermitage in the remote mountains of Big Sur, California. I saw him regularly in confession for years. Once he told me that sex is a mystery. I knew I had heard the definitive four words on sex.

Last night my wife and I celebrated my birthday, celebrated with a married couple who lives in our condominium. They took us next door to another party, a happy lively party made up of about thirty gay men. One of my sons, a good man, had been gay; he died of AIDS at forty-two.

I wrote this chapter years before the emergence of LGBTQ into popular consciousness. Rather than rewriting it now I'll remind you that in humanity and the rest of the animal kingdom the great majority of sexual beings are heterosexual. Please forgive me should what I go on to say or fail to say leaves you wanting.

There was darkness on the deep, a vaginal archetype if I ever did see one. And then the creation, with energetic Light entering into the picture. Rather phallic, don't you think?

So, in the beginning was the vagina. In the beginning of the creation, that is, in the beginning of the story; but before that was whoever made the damn thing.

From the scientific point of view, rather than the biblical one, a lot of hot gases were swirling around a long time ago, and when they cooled down you had rock and water.

Just a ball of hot rock and water spinning around in the cosmos, and nothing was ever added to it, from a scientific point of view.

Big bang. And the next thing you knew, presto, there was a VAGINA. How the heck did that get there? Was there a vagina hiding in the rock and water from the beginning? Nothing added, and the next thing you know, something soft, often smelly, goes from dry to moist, hidden, drives men crazy.

The first time I sensed there were vaginas around was right after graduating from my wrought-iron-fenced kindergarten yard and going onto the broader fields of first grade, playground fields shared by all six grades at Alta Loma Elementary School.

There were monkey bars on that bigger schoolyard. Monkey bars were made up of six fifteen-foot metal poles that were joined at the top in a tight metal hub, but whose legs were spread out and stuck in the ground, just like those of a large Indian tepee. The kids climbed those monkey bars, climbed them all the way to the top. Sometimes they just hung on them high off the ground, like little monkeys.

That is, the other kids climbed them. I stayed on the ground. I was afraid of heights. I just stayed on the ground and watched.

I don't remember seeing the boys climb. But I do remember the girls. The girls had white panties under their dresses. I had never seen under girls' dresses before (I didn't learn everything I needed to know in kindergarten). The girls' smooth and shapely little girl legs led right up to that inviting and delicious patch that was alluringly and mysteriously covered with white cotton panties.

First grade. Education. The discovery of little girls' white panties.

And I stayed on the ground and looked up their dresses at that smooth and lively covered patch for at least a school year, and nobody had told me to do that, and nobody had told me I could do that. I didn't even know why I was doing it. It was not only natural for me; it was compelling.

God had given me a feel for the magnetism vaginas weave on most little boys' eyes and bodies. I was six years old.

I KNEW WHEN I woke this morning (I am eighty again and not six) I'd be writing more about vaginas, I just didn't know what exactly, and I was still dazed by a long night's sleep in which I dreamed of a pleasant visit from my long dead mother, from whose vagina I had once magically emerged.

On my way outdoors to get the morning paper two things happened in rapid succession, and together they awakened my sleep-groggy and vulnerable mind.

First, I saw a beautifully open red and purple flower right about eye level in the morning sunlight. It was riding on a graceful bright green stem. My wife had put it there on a plant stand in our sun porch, the room we go through on our way to the great outdoors.

The flower looked ever so vaginal, more so to one sleepily thinking about vaginas. I took it as a bracing message from the creator of flowers and vaginas, a creator (if there is a creator) who can pull them both out of a swirling ball of rock and water in staggering numbers whenever he wishes, easier than a magician pulls rabbits out of a hat.

The second awakening thing was a sharp, high-pitched sound above my head, like a toot from the horn of a Model A Ford. I looked up to see a fast-flying duck go by less than twenty feet off the ground. It went right over my head. Another miracle! Especially to one not yet desensitized by the day's commerce, traffic, and television. The duck was a mallard, brown with a brown head. Not the iridescent purple and green head of the male. It was a female mallard.

A sign from God! A flying vagina! Now that I think of it, there must be at least billions of vaginas flying around the earth at any given instant. Heavenly. And that's not even counting those riding in airplanes or on the space station.

Then there are the vaginas under the earth: gopher vaginas, mole vaginas, shrew vaginas, prairie dog vaginas; and all the temporarily underground vaginas of the animals that sleep in burrows, like fox vaginas, mouse vaginas, badger vaginas.

Vaginas in rivers and ponds, lakes and streams: beaver, otter, and the cold vagina salmon.

Vaginas under the oceans: teeming schools of vaginas in fish, and the warm- or hot-blooded vaginas of seals and sea lions, walruses, dolphins and whales.

To repeat:

In the air above us, flying vaginas.

In the sea around us, a wondrous array of hot and cold vaginas spinning and schooling and circling in deep watery space.

In the ground below us, tunneling vaginas (the vagina itself a mysterious sort of tunnel, and all tunnels are therefore mysterious, and take their mystery from her).

And then there are the vaginas that move, either horizontally or vertically, on top of the ground, our own earthy level:

The cat vagina, dog vagina, polar bear vagina, gecko vagina, elephant vagina, giraffe vagina, hamster vagina. Go ahead, keep naming them.

Imagine all the dusty vaginas in a dry-weather stampede of wildebeests. All the wet vaginas in great flocks of migrating geese leaving Canada.

Not to mention the vaginas of years gone by: Saber-tooth tiger vaginas. Countless dinosaur vaginas. Mastodon vaginas. The vaginas of pterodactyls. Once they thrilled to the compelling tinglings and deeper currents of sex. Now only moldering memories that cling to old bones in museum show rooms.

To paraphrase a great statement of Abraham Lincoln, God must have loved the vagina, because he made so many of them.

I CAN'T AVOID TALKING about that delicate and central subject any longer: The vaginas of grown women.

Especially the vagina of a woman who is physically capable of sexual relations. One of those vaginas that might take part in an orgasm. The sort of vagina we usually see before her hair turns gray. The easily moistened kind. The sort of vagina that serves as curtains for baby's first bow. The sweetest sort of vagina.

Here are two stories:

I witnessed the first about ten or fifteen years ago, the last time miniskirts were in fashion: the skirt that makes some women look like goddesses and others like clowns.

I was standing in a bank line, waiting to make a deposit, waiting with a number of other mildly bored people, and I was looking around for anything to take my mind off the time passing slowly, when in walked a beautiful young woman, fashionably dressed in a high-cut miniskirt that revealed her dazzling tanned legs.

She was accompanied by a good-looking but sawed-off male who looked to be around six years of age, handsome, virile, fresh out of kindergarten.

His head came up to somewhere not far above her knees.

From the look of this couple, and the way they treated each other, I knew I was watching a mother and son. The love was there. And the training.

The little boy kept running his hand up his mother's inner thigh and under her skirt, and she let him, but only to a few inches of the point where he'd be touching the spot that God makes so central in his earthly creation. No, she stopped him right there, just before his fingers got THERE.

She stopped him over and over again. He was persistent. She was persistent. I felt in time she was going to win the conflict, and he was going to quit trying, at least with her.

And after a while, he did quit.

I commend you, Mother, whoever and wherever you are. You knew what your son wanted to do. You knew you weren't going to let him do it. You used your superior size and strength to set your limits. But in a very loving, gentle and firm way. You showed no anger, no irritation, or worse yet, revulsion or horror. You engendered no shame in your son, and no anxiety.

When your training was over the boy continued to know what he wanted to do, felt all right about wanting to do it, just knew he couldn't do it. Kind of like the kid who quite naturally wants to stay up past bedtime but knows it's not in his six-year-old cards.

But because of our society's rather widespread revulsion with a boy's sexual curiosity and attraction toward his mother, many youngsters do not leave this stage of their training without certain damages having been visited on their interior.

And my second story, which is longer and more complex than the first, concerns just this sort of unhealthy revulsion and outcome: The man in question, once a boy, was a client of mine. He was very well-endowed physically and always well-groomed; he looked like a mid-twentieth-century movie star, tall, athletic, and graceful, in the manner of Henry Fonda or Jimmy Stewart. Actually his name was Rodney, or, as he preferred, Rod.

Rod was forty-five years old. He enjoyed a solid, lifelong skilled career and was well-employed in a large business. He showed up to work on time. He paid his bills on time. He was pleasant and non-abrasive. Rod was what has come to be called, to my dismay and anger, a functioning member of society.

Rod came into psychotherapy with me seeking relief from his chronic and painful depression. As with so many depressed people, his pain didn't show. He exemplified what Freud meant by Neurosis: everyone thinks you're doing just fine, but you know you're feeling miserable inside.

Rod was a lifelong bachelor but had entered into large numbers of sexual encounters, including several affairs that lasted a year or so. He had also lived with two of those women.

About half of his briefest sexual encounters (the one-night stands) had been with women; the other half had been with men. This feature of his life history emerged slowly. The sort of trust it required him to reveal his bisexuality is seldom developed within the limits of today's highly touted short-term therapy.

Rod had been bisexual since adolescence. In spite of an outwardly normal appearance, he led a rather sad and isolated life, with no real friends. His only living relative was a brother, five years older, who lived a few hundred miles away.

This brother had forced sex upon Rod during the years just before his adolescence, but Rod demonstrated little feeling about the event, and actually very little feeling about any of his sexual history.

Sex for him was almost purely erotic and physical. There was never much sense of a caring relationship in it. Most of his encounters with men were one-night stands. The two current exceptions were his brother, with whom he coupled occasionally, and a past employer, who although married and putting on a faithful face to his wife and the world, snuck out at times to service and be serviced by Rod, and this over a period of years.

Rod's relations with women, even the ones he had lived with, were at best those of friendly acquaintances. There was no depth of feeling, and no real emotional involvement. When it was time to leave them he left easily.

And so he was lonely. And so he longed for marriage. But somehow, probably at a time before his memory began, the link between sex and love had been broken. Love for him signaled sexual disinterest and impotence.

We talked a lot about this problem: that he was highly erotic, but could not connect his sexual drive to his heart. We went back again and again to his childhood. His father had been away much of the time, busy in a career that involved travel and therefore lengthy absences from home. His mother stayed and parented him and his brother. She was consistently described as sweet, nurturing and maternal. In later years, father switched careers and no longer traveled. Then the loud and violent marital wars began, and lasted until his parents' divorce, when my client was in his early teens.

After close to a year had passed in therapy, with slow but real progress in his mood disorder, I asked him to bring any photographs he had of his childhood, and he brought in the four or five he could find.

In one photograph he is three years old, standing alone with his mother during some sort of country outing. They are standing rather side by side, a short distance apart. He is already tall for his age and good-looking. There are park-like trees all about them. And mother, wearing a black silhouette dress, is ravishing.

Take the little boy out of the picture and you have a classic pin-up photo, a movie-star pose for a horny sailor's locker during World War II. She's got what it takes. She radiates pizzazz, beauty, and sexuality. I am instantly responsive.

In a while I gather my response into professionally appropriate terms and communicate something of how I feel about and see her, the mother he has always only described as soft, nurturing, and maternal.

He doesn't know what I'm talking about.

I put it to him more directly.

He doesn't know what I'm talking about.

I am altogether direct.

He still doesn't know what I'm talking about.

It turns out that whenever Rod looked at this picture he failed to see his mother's body. He saw himself. He saw the park-like trees. He saw his mother's head and face. But where her body is he doesn't really quite know what he sees. Maybe nothing. Or maybe a blur. This is how he always sees this picture; but until this point in time he did not know that this is how he sees this picture. He was unconscious of editing out all reference to his mother's sexuality, any signposts pointing toward her ovaries, womb, and vagina.

And so it went: with a photo or without a photo, Rod could see nothing, hear nothing, speak nothing, of his mother's sexuality. As far as he was concerned, mother and sexuality, mother and vagina, had nothing to do with one another. But the photo spoke otherwise, to everyone but Rod.

The therapy, which now went on to include the recovery of sensibilities that our first little boy, the one with his mother in the bank line, never lost, was a relative success. Forty-five-year-old Rod eventually did fall in love with a woman: a woman his own age, a woman named Linda, a woman who reciprocated his love. It was the first time he had fallen in love with anyone.

Linda and Rod had known each other a long time, having worked together for years. I suppose the healing he was undergoing during therapy helped take their relationship to what for both was reported to be a new and magical level of romance.

After some months the love between them was consummated, and they began to enjoy a rousing good sex life, far better and more wondrous than either could remember having before. Rod felt his heart and penis working as a team. His depression lifted. He was happy, monogamous. Faithful.

But she was not. Married for twenty years, including all the years she had known Rod, Linda continued sexual relations with her husband, who Rod reported was a cold and unemotional man, and that according to his beloved's account.

From a therapist's perspective, Rod had improved but had yet to completely solve his problem. He had come close to melding love and sexuality; but there was still the fact of the illegitimacy of his current relationship: he couldn't phone Linda at home when hubby was there, couldn't be publicly demonstrative with her, couldn't have Linda without sharing her with another man: all the usual and sad impediments of adultery.

I told Rod I thought he was still feeling unconsciously guilty about having sexual relations with the woman he loved, and that he'd unconsciously set up this romance to have something bad (his lover's marital infidelity) woven in close to its center.

So Rod, who was never much given to conscious guilt, did the decent thing, from his perspective, and left psychotherapy. And I haven't heard or seen from him since. Not one of my more spectacular therapeutic successes, but it still serves to illustrate some problematic sexual realities.

WHEN MOST OF US chaps are tadpoles, say three to six years of age, Mommy is the most important woman in our lives. We need her, feel we really can't live without her. And we see her as stupendously beautiful (watch a happy six-year-old looking at Mommy).

Then what if this supremely lovable and essential-to-our-happiness-and-security goddess puts the kibosh on our sexual drive when it's quite naturally and inevitably aimed at her? Gives us that You Nasty Boy Feeling! Doesn't handle our sexual and amorous expressions like Mommy-in-the-bank-line did. Slaps our hand away. Scares the hell out of us. Treats us coldly (I only love you when you're a nice little eunuch).

It really doesn't take long at all, doesn't take much, to give us the feeling that if we long to know more about Mommy's pussy we are either heading for big trouble, bad boys, or both.

That's different than Mommy won't let me run my hand all the way up to where her legs join and let me feel around, but I'm O.K. for really wanting to, just that the answer is no.

HAS ANYONE THOUGHT OF the Virgin Mary yet? She's been in the back of my mind all along, and in my heart, too. What a beautiful woman. Makes me think of my mother-in-law, who is the second saint I've known personally. Well, in a way we're all saints, because if there's a heaven we all end up there. But my mother-in-law is a saint because she's so close to being ready for heaven right now. Maybe a little rust that needs to be brushed off, maybe a little dust, but I can't see it.

Coincidentally, the other saint I've known was a woman, too. Her name was Ma Watkins. Like my mother-in-law, Ma had chosen to stick by and raise a number of children after her husband died. Like my mother-in-law, Ma was part Native American. And like my mother-in law, Ma's child-rearing years had held unending work and unending material poverty.

I met Ma when I was about seven. The youngest of her ten children, Albert Watkins, was about to marry my live-in babysitter, Rose Katzenellenbogen. Al was a plumber from a small beach town in California. He was proud to be an eighth-part Cherokee and proud to have been a star high school athlete in every sport you could name. His skin was dark and reddish, and his hair was black and full and straight, and he laughed all the time, and was always nice to me.

My babysitter, Rose, was about six feet tall, beautiful, with long, thick, wavy black hair. She and her two sisters had been raised by their mother, very poor, in Brooklyn. Rose loved to jitterbug. And she had been the only girl to play on the high school boys' varsity basketball team when her family moved to San Francisco.

Ma Watkins loved her son, Al. She loved her new daughter-in-law-to-be, Rose. She loved me. Maybe she loved everyone. Ma had a large wart growing on her nose. It was the same color as the rest of her dark and reddish-brown skin. The wart looked like it had been on Ma's nose a long, long time. I asked Rose about it, and she got mad at me, said she just knew I was going to ask.

The summer after I met Ma I lost Rose, because Rose married Al, left Los Angeles, and moved about 40 miles south to Huntington Beach. They lived in one of a short row of old former oil-worker cabins Al was buying, and on the back of the property he had set up his plumbing supplies and shop. Ma lived in the cabin next to theirs.

Then when I was ten I got Rose back. I went to live with her and Al for the summer. And I lived there every summer for the next six years. So I had a lot of time to know Ma Watkins, and I even lived in her cabin with her for days at time.

Ma Watkins had a deep, melodic, older woman's voice, full of the soft resonances and easy cadences of rural Tennessee, and full of the sweetness that only sainthood brings. She laughed just about all the time. And she cried easily, too. She talked a lot and listened well. She never acted or put on a pose. Her skin was leathery like a fine, soft glove. She loved me and served me. And she talked and sang about Jesus much of the day, every day.

I also remember the breakfasts she made me. Bacon and eggs that were hot and greasy and succulent to the point of mystery. No woman had ever been so loving to me.

When I think about Ma now I just get warm inside and smile to myself, a little sad that I'll never see her again this side of the grave. I was so young when I met her, so inexperienced, that I didn't realize I might never come across her like again.

And then many years after Ma died I did meet her like again, Nellie Lee Parker, my mother-in-law, so much like Ma Watkins, and like Ma, a saint, the second one I've met. Only now that I know how rare saints are, and how we might meet none at all in a lifetime, or one or two at the average most, I take the time to appreciate her while she still walks this earth.

She is eighty-eight years old now, and lives on the farmland in rural Alabama that her parents owned, the land she grew up on, and the land she returned to and raised her six children after her husband died.

She had been a virgin, and a very pretty laughing woman, when she married in her middle twenties. She married an extremely tall man: her husband Mark was six-eight or six-nine. Mark was a lumberjack and sawmill worker. The endless woods around the valley farmland they lived on were rich with pine. On weekends Mark played the piano at some of the clubs in town, and his nickname was Flash.

This was Nellie's first real love and these were happy years for both of them, and for their children. Mark had a health problem, though: a bleeding ulcer. One night it got so bad that he saddled both their mules to the wagon and went off to the hospital for some much-needed medical help.

The doctors knew what was wrong with Mark and they knew just what to do. Because this was a white hospital, and Mark was a black man, they did the decent thing and sent him off to the nearest black people's hospital, which was twenty miles down the dirt road. Sent him off on his wagon drawn by two mules. And he bled to death on the way.

Nellie's six children ranged from nine months to sixteen years old when their father died. There were two girls and four boys. They moved back to Nellie's parents' farm, and she raised them there in a one-bedroom house next to her parents' home. That house was almost hurricane-proof because the wind just went through it; the wallboards weren't that close together.

Nellie worked in a laundry, and she walked quite a ways to and from work every day. When she got back home in the early evening she often rode off in a truck with other laborers to pick the cotton fields while the light lasted. Her children hated to see her go.

She made breakfast for them every morning and saw to it they all had bag lunches for their noon meal. She cooked and canned and had their suppers going on time. She laughed with them, switched them with a switch when they needed it, got them to church with her every Sunday.

Now one of her sons is a retired university professor in Florida; two are retired from middle management positions with General Motors in Detroit; and one is retired as athletic director at a university in Alabama.

We see each other together mostly when we see Nellie, who is their mother, and whom I call Mother, and whom it turns out most everyone who knows her secretly feels is their mother.

Nellie is fun to be with, and when you are near her you just feel better and better until you are feeling so good it is hard to contain yourself. You will be laughing with her and you won't know why. Even if she is telling you about how her back has been hurting, for some reason you will be feeling better and better; even if she's telling you about her allergies.

It is an honor when she asks you to chop her firewood. But when you're almost done she'll appear on the back porch and watch you a while, and when you're spent, she'll pick up the ax and chop a while herself, and you'll realize she knows more about chopping wood than you ever will, and that she knows it in some deep spot that is deeper than any spot you've discovered in yourself.

Nellie Lee Parker, Mother Parker . . . Mother, is a saint.

All day long she goes around the house singing church choir music, doing all the solo parts and all the choir parts, and never missing a note, song after song. It is a joyful sound.

I'll bet the Virgin Mary had beautiful hands, just like in all the pictures of her. But after that, most of her resemblance to those pictures ends. Because the Virgin Mary looked real Jewish. I mean *real* Jewish. The kind of girl whose family can't join the country club. The kind of girl you stopped inviting to your birthday parties. The Bible tells me so.

And not just Jewish like we know it now, but Jewish like it was then: more like Korean is now, where all the Koreans look the same because there is hardly any intermarriage in Korea and the racial stock is pretty darn pure.

So to know what Mary looked like you have to picture some racially pure Arab-type woman, some dark-ass desert dweller. If Mary had been light-skinned and blondish like the European ad companies make her out to be, why that would have been so physically remarkable that the Bible would have mentioned it, like it does with the hairy red-bearded Esau, the giant-sized Goliath, or the woolly white-haired guy in Revelations.

No, Mary had a few-thousand-year string of Jewish mommies and daddies, all the way back to Adam and Eve. So you can bet she was brown-skinned, dark-eyed, and black-haired, with full lips, and though her nose might be small, it was a Jewish nose.

Born without sin, ever so radiant, and a joy to be around. Awful pretty, because her genes made up half of Jesus's genetic makeup. And the owner, historically speaking, of the cutest, sweetest, and most loving pussy in the history of creation. With smooth and shiny black pubic hair framing the soft skin that the sun had never darkened.

Before I go on to further discuss the most important vagina in the cosmos, the vagina that belongs to the most saintly woman in history, I need to make an observation about our attitude towards the English language. I need to do this so I can talk comfortably and clearly about the Virgin Mary's pussy, or, if you will, her vagina. The observation I need to make about our attitude toward the English language is that when we feel something is indecent and off-limits we use a Latin or Greek word for it.

Take *cunt*, for example. Our society, or at least many of its members, and especially Praetorians, members of the Sanhedrin, and all those who follow them blindly, decry the word *cunt*. It is O.K. to talk about *vaginas*, because that is a very Latinate form and has three syllables, but it is not O.K. to say *cunt* because that is pure old Anglo-Saxon, and only has one syllable.

Geoffrey Chaucer, who wrote *Canterbury Tales*, the greatest Catholic book of all time, other than the Bible, used words like *cunt*. He also said *turd* instead of *feces*. *Feces* is a Latinate word. *Turd* is an Anglo-Saxon word. And so it goes. We say *urine* because it's a Latin term and has two syllables, and not the word that says the same thing, *piss*, because that's Anglo-Saxon and only one syllable. And besides, it's decent to talk about urination, but indecent to talk about pissing, even though the two root words mean exactly the same thing.

When we have to go to Greek you know there's something being said that we'd rather not understand at all: like the word *psychotherapy*. Very Greek that, from the Greek words *psyche* and *therapos*, meaning soul and healing, respectively.

Soul? Wait, we don't recognize the existence of a soul, do we? And healing? Wouldn't that imply the soul might be sick?

You mean I'm seeing a soul healer to have my sick soul healed? Tell me it isn't true. Let's call it psychotherapy, make me think it's scientific rather than spiritual, and if I'm not better in two weeks give me Prozac.

By the way, when I ran my computer's spell check on this passage it failed to recognize the words *cunt*, *turd* and *piss*. I had to add them. It knew *vagina*, *feces*, and *urine*, though. Such a nice, decent spell check, and now I've gone and corrupted it, much in the manner of Socrates.

And now a true story on many indecent words.

The time is 1967. The place is one of the most affluent sections of Orange County, California. Affluent and proper. Fresh white paint. Republican. Coiffed hair. Suit and tie. Decent.

I worked in Orange County as a soul healer, mostly in one of its public mental health clinics, but also in part-time private practice for the rich folks.

A lady psychologist who only served rich folks was doing marathon group therapy now and then and invited me to join as her co-therapist. The pay for a day was more than I made in a week, and the new mode of therapy was being praised in the papers and periodicals, so I willingly climbed aboard to see all about it.

Our marathon therapy regularly got ten or twelve customers into her large and luxurious office at 7:30 in the evening and kept them doing therapy together for twenty-four hours, with breaks every four hours for communal eating from a sumptuous buffet. Participants could use the bathroom as needed. No sleeping, though. Basically it was just nonstop round-the clock group therapy.

I was a marathon therapy therapist on six separate occasions, and it was grueling and I was tired for days afterwards; then I'd had enough and stopped, even though some of the results had been most impressive.

The good thing about marathon therapy is that it speeds up the process of people getting real with each other, because very few people can keep their masks on for twenty-four hours without sleeping or leaving each other's company. So if someone is always afraid to take off the mask of her fake smile, or if someone is afraid to take off his mask of always acting nothing but charitable, or nothing but macho, and it's really just a mask, and something sadder or more selfish or softer is going on underneath, then by God a marathon is going to get them to put that mask down from the pure fatigue of holding it in place so long, and they're going to see how the real them gets along with other folks, and it's probably going to be much better than they ever thought possible.

Another thing that happened every time in marathon therapy was a change in language, and the change in language always began about four o'clock in the morning when someone in the conservative Orange County of that era said a dirty word.

The dirty word would just slip out of a crack in someone's mask of gentility and properness and show its rather innocent self to the assembled group.

Like some guy might say *pussy* instead of *vagina*, and then one or more people in the group would attack him for saying *pussy* instead of *vagina*, and maybe one or two people would defend him for saying *pussy* instead of *vagina*. And then the group would go on another half-hour and someone would say *fuck*. And then we'd have another heated attack and defense of that word, but this time with more people joining in, and this second discussion would go on a bit longer than the first, and when it was over the group would go back to whatever issues it was working on.

And by eight o'clock every morning everyone in the group was saying *pussy* and *vagina*, and *fuck* and *sexual intercourse*, and picking whichever word felt right at the time, and nobody gave a shit, or a feces anymore, because a word was just a word, which is what a word is, you know.

I just added *shit* to my spell-check. But all these words are already in the Oxford English Dictionary. They are words. Freedom of speech.

Jesus noted that it ain't what we put into our mouths that makes us unclean, it's the words that come out of our mouths, because they tell what our hearts are like. I don't think he meant words like *pussy* and *fuck*, unless they were being spoken in a mean context. I think he meant words like, "We better suppress that report on the toxic effects of tobacco or the public won't buy our cigarettes." Or, "Here's the list of synagogues and churches we're going to firebomb." Or, "We can't give the workers thirty days notice or they may slow production down." Words like that.

So HERE IS THIS extra extra beautiful vagina, the most significant vagina in history, and we never see pictures of it, and probably most people don't want to think about it much, but I think not thinking about it much has helped to keep us in all the trouble we're in: wars everywhere, pollution, global warming, poverty, and all the other human behavior that seems to indicate so convincingly that humanity is cursed with something originally, enduringly, and pervasively sinful in its nature.

And speaking of original sin, there's another very important vagina in history: Eve's. As soon as she and Adam sinned, Eve covered up her vagina. Even so we have a lot of pictures of Eve running around pretty naked.

If you believe there's just this life, and no heaven, then Eve's vagina is the one for you. Lately the scientists, of all people, are saying there really was an Eve, one lady that we all descended from. They say this from what they understand about human DNA.

Well, whenever a little girl is born, her little vagina means that someone might be coming out of it in a decade or three. And if that someone is a woman, and has a vagina, then someone might be coming out of her. And so it goes. Kind of a great chain of being. You know, the latest vagina came out of a vagina that came out of another vagina, and it came out of yet another vagina, and so on, all the way back to the original Eve.

But if it's a little boy, well, that's the end of the line. Nothing visible is ever coming out of him, except maybe a little sperm. Another person is never going to come out of him. A little boy is a creative dud that way. He emerges from a vagina that emerged from a vagina that emerged from a vagina all the way back to Eve. But nothing is ever going to emerge from him but a little sperm.

If you're a woman, another person might grow inside you and emerge, and if it's another woman, well and good. We can keep on going.

So, Eve, whom we tend to think of as sexy, is about the continuation of the race, about a sort of immortality for the species as a whole, but not for us as individuals. Matter of fact, we're each going to die because of the trouble she got us into; but if we don't neutron bomb everyone out of existence in the same moment, then Eve, the biological mother of us all, has a part in our kids, grandkids, and their kids keeping you and me going as long as the human race does, but at most as highly remote memories.

We all know Eve is our mother, and the original bad girl. Plus her and Adam couldn't have been all that happy. They lost their home and everything, had two children and one of them ended up murdering the other. Eve is rather bad news. It's O.K. to feel sexy about Eve. Show her tits. Show her ass. Show her naked all the time. O.K., put a G-string or a fig leaf on her privates; we'll still know they're there, like a massage parlor girl or a stripper (or the little girls on the monkey poles). Even though Eve's our mother, it's O.K. to feel sexual because she's a bad girl, a bad woman; there's something wrong with her. Just like Linda, Rod's first love.

The Virgin Mary, on the other hand, is the original good girl. The Immaculate Conception is not a term used for Jesus. The Immaculate Conception is a term used for Mary. It means she was born without the effects of the original sin that Eve and Adam committed. She was exempted from it.

All the rest of us biological offspring of Adam and Eve have been strug-gling with their sin the same way children are born into a national debt that they didn't run up. Just look at the history of wars and the sinful dis-crepancies between the very rich and very poor to see we're all fucked up. That started with Eve and Adam's mistake, the effects of which have spread throughout the cosmos.

Mary wasn't fucked up at all. Mary was just good. Immaculate Concep-tion. I guess God made her that way because he wanted a suitable womb to grow in before he parted the waves of her perfectly beautiful vagina and entered this glorious and woebegone world of ours.

Fine. She was all good. That doesn't mean she wasn't sexual. Neither she nor Jesus was born without a sex drive. But we go down through the centuries denying the fact of her sexuality. We dress her in long thick robes of blue, a pretty and cold color, trimmed with white, another color not noted for its warmth. We hide her dark-skinned legs that were, let's face it, shapely and strong. We hide her curvy and attractive body.

She's Mother. But not Mother of the young boy in the bank line. Not Al Watkins's Mother when she was young and sexually attractive. Not Nellie Lee Parker when six-nine Mark Parker gave up his free bachelor ways forever for the love of her.

Nope. She's Rod's asexual mother, before he was close to being able to stay in love and be sexually aroused at the same time. We're not allowed to know how sexy we feel about her. Do you think Saint Joseph ever knew? Or was he just after her for her money?

So the Virgin Mary isn't real. Or, more accurately, our picture of her isn't real. Doesn't conform to human reality. No wonder so many people have trouble believing she ever really existed. And no wonder so many folks have trouble feeling sexual with the woman they most need and love.

When Wife becomes like Mother once was for us, the supremely most important and lovable woman in our life, our childhood training may unconsciously tell us that good fucking is now taboo.

Good fucking, by the way, happens when both people's sexual organs are connected to their loving hearts: hence, the apt term, lovemaking. Good fucking and lovemaking are both three-syllable terms, and neither has any Latin or Greek to them. To hell with sexual intercourse.

Maybe that's why men like boobs so much. Cause when they were little infants and were hot for Mom's breasts most of them were never made to feel frightened or bad about their fervent desires. Go ahead, son, feel it. Suck on it. You know you want it. You know you need it. Looks good. Is good. Yummie. Oh, Mommy!

They're always painting the Virgin's breasts into pictures; well, one breast anyway, and making it look attractive.

WE ALSO HIDE THE down-to-earth reality of the most important event in history, the birth and incarnation of God. We do this by calling an entirely different event the Nativity Scene, nativity being the four-syllable Latin word for birth, and then don't show a birth at all: We show a baby who was born quite a few minutes ago, because someone has had time to clean him up, dress him up, lie him down, and he usually looks about three or four months old.

I have witnessed three real-life nativity scenes and been present at two real-life births, and the two things are very different. Births are better. You learn more at them. You grow more. And they are much harder to describe, especially the way your soul goes off like Old Faithful at Yellowstone, like meteor showers, and like fireworks at night in the Coliseum. I am not saying births are like this for the mother, because she is in so much pain and discomfort most of the time.

The first three children I fathered involved nativity scenes because back then the doctors wouldn't let Dad be there when his wife opened up her legs and a new human being sloshed onto this side of the grave.

I had to stay in the waiting room with the other Saint Josephs, and after hours went by, the nurse came and led me to a wall with a large glass panel mounted into it, and through that glass darkly I could see a room full of clear plastic baskets with newborn babies inside them, and one plastic basket had our last name taped to it. And the child was wrapped in swaddling clothes. And I felt a rush of something, joy and adoration.

But I have also been to two birth scenes, the births of my last two children. Because the doctors, who had not been running things at the manger in Bethlehem—God couldn't afford them?—allowed me to be present when these births occurred. I could sit beside my wife, hold her hand, look into her eyes, talk with her. I got to see the wonder of what lovemaking could bring.

Both times the wonder arrived amidst shit and piss. A doctor friend of mine once quoted a medical saying about this phenomenon. It was in Latin, of course, for delicacy's sake, but roughly translated: "Amidst shit and piss we are born, and amidst shit and piss we die." Probably said *feces* and *urine*, but I think that robs the language of its impact.

And the sight of shit pouring out of the hole below my wife's vagina, and the sight of piss pouring out of the hole above my wife's vagina, had a shocking impact, a great earthy and at the same time cosmic and miraculous overture to the spreading vaginal lips opening to applaud the head of the star of that moment's show. And then out he stepped. And the roller coaster loop of it, the lightning charge of it: to be present at, and witness to, a real miracle. That changes a guy forever.

Just as Saint Joseph was changed. Or do you think the cows and sheep attended Mary during her labor? Or do you think Joe averted his eyes when the woman he loved hiked her skirts up? Get real, people. Joe might have gone out for a short smoke break during the Nativity Scene, but he was there with his beloved when she spread her legs to make way for the Lord of Lords. And there was shit and piss, too. Holy shit. And there was Mary's sweet vagina. And there was Mary's holy, loving, motherly, wifely heart. And her holy heart and her holy vagina were connected. And everything was connected. She was without sin. She was whole.

I believe it's time for more of our artists to tackle this reality. If God grants us another full millennium, let's see them try the Virgin birth. Art was first and best defined by Aristotle: art is something which both delights and teaches. We've been taught enough this past millennium about the well-wrapped baby with people and dumb animals kneeling around him; also about a sweet mother with one sweet breast out near baby's hand and mouth. I think the artists may have exhausted these themes. The museum walls are lined with them. We get it. We got it. We like it.

But there's something more. Something about the wonder of birth rather than the wonder of baby in his first blanket. Please step up to the palette.

The artists could deal not only with the awakening shock of what the birth of Jesus really was like, but also the awakening shock of what Mary and the baby really looked like: Not English, Dutch, or German, not even northern Italian. Nope, they were Jewish folks and they looked like Jews back then, before all the mixing. Arab-like. Dark hair. Dark eyes. Dark skin.

Look at the baby's nose. So cute and tiny. Won't grow and begin to hook until he reaches puberty.

DO YOU KNOW WHAT Freud and all the other soul-healers after him said about denial? Denial is when you stuff some reality down into your unconscious because for some reason the reality you stuffed is just too painful for you to handle consciously.

An alcoholic or a cigarette addict often goes into denial about the severity of his addiction. Denial looks very smooth and unruffled on the surface.

"I had a couple of beers last night."

"How many is a couple?"

"A six-pack."

"You seem to be smoking every time I see you."

"I could quit any time I wanted to."

The hallmark of denial is that when it's attacked the person in denial gets furious at you. Here's an example of what I mean.

I was trying to help a lady whose husband had been beating her up with regularity. After an interview or two with her I asked to meet him. He arrived, a stocky muscular young man with very white skin and very dark hair. The hair was thick and fairly long, but plastered back and straight with some sort of glossy hair oil. He was just a touch unshaven, and his prominent jaw was blue-black with stubble.

He was wearing tight jeans, and a black cotton T-shirt with a pack of cigarettes rolled up in one sleeve. He carried the butt of an unlit well-chewed cigar in his hand and used it for emphasis when he spoke to me. He also carried a well-developed sense of menace about him.

After our time together loosened up, and he saw I wasn't out to get him, he went into a rather long soliloquy about his habit of standing in the shadows outside gay bars, and, when the time was right, decking some emerging and unfortunate gay male victim, preferably cold-cocking him to the hard and unforgiving sidewalk. This was his sport, and he told me about it with relish, studying me for my reaction.

He made it very clear that he harbored hatred for all gay men, and expressed this hatred by visiting their habitat and hunting and destroying them.

I felt sure that the man was having trouble with his own sense of masculinity, enough to drive him to costume himself as a macho stereotype, and enough to be anguished by his own probably unconscious homosexual feelings and impulses. He was angry with what was going on inside of himself, but that was too painful for him to look at, and so he projected outward and punished others, in this case guys who were all too visibly gay.

This was only my fourth year as a therapist, and I had already lost one front tooth to someone's fist, so I took the coward's way out and never asked if he thought he himself might be harboring some elements of homosexuality. Nor did I see myself pressing him, arguing with him if he said something like, "No way." What I did see was that given my limited skills of that time, I would most likely get knocked out of my chair if I pressed the matter of his yearnings for sex with other men. I chose discretion as the better part of valor.

Our culture is in denial about a number of significant realities. It would be healthier if we faced up to whatever pain we feel, and in the process face up to the reality we don't want to look at.

The Virgin birth involved, like all births of the time, a woman with her legs apart, pubic hair, a vagina. There was a guy around, a guy who loved the woman. The guy looked Jewish because he was Jewish. Likewise the young woman.

I've seen a painting of just this event on the wall of a small coffee house in Santa Barbara. The artist had brought something beautiful to the birth scene by his use of circular forms underlying much of the anatomy: the baby's emerging head, the virgin's head, and to a lesser extent, circular forms defining her legs, torso, and arms. The artist wasn't that good, but there was a combination of the historical and cosmic that I liked, and no one was cleaned up and blanketed. It was a start.

When we won't tell it like it is, when we won't know it like it is, when what it really was like and really looked like feels just too revolting and unacceptable to us, when the first saints' Jewishness and the need for a young pussy to be present at the redemptive moment become painfully intolerable to us, we lose the mysterious historical reality of the Gospels and slide down the long slope that leads to plaster manikin statues and images of the latest young movies stars. It's part of our way of saying that the whole thing never happened, or that it only happened the way we wish it would have, both of which wishes are lies. These lies help keep husbands the world over highly attracted to their mistresses rather than their wives, and people the world over blaming everything on the Jews.

BEFORE THE CHRISTIANS CAME to stay with them Samoan Islanders were doing fine with sex, and many other things. This was partly because, unlike us, they didn't make mother such a super special person to the child to whom she had given birth. The child was generally raised by everyone in the village, cared for especially by folks in the mother's hut, which is to say somewhere between twelve and twenty-four other people, but mommy was just one of the family, and not that special to the kid, or that sexually taboo, either.

In fact, sex itself wasn't that taboo. The three or four couples in the hut would go at sex with nothing covering them but a small canopy of mosquito netting. Anyone who wanted to look on could do so, and the kids did. Meanwhile the premarital adolescents were off in the jungle at various hours, especially evenings, involving themselves in short-lived affairs of fucking and sucking, and the little kids sported to watch their slightly older relatives having at it.

The Samoans were, shall we say, more natural in other ways as well. Births were witnessed by whoever wanted to watch, so everyone was familiar with childbirth, too, and realized that vaginas, shit, and piss were involved, and that is just the way things are.

The same goes for death and dying. They were not taking place off in secret, or with a few of the closest relatives in attendance. They were more of a community event. Things just weren't all that hidden in Samoa until the Christians came along. People in Samoa saw more of life's earthiest realities in one week than most of us do in an entire lifetime.

You may think this all very primitive and benighted of these pre-Christian folk. But the Samoans didn't have any fathers screwing their daughters and swearing them to secrecy, no pornographic industry growing stronger every day, no prostitution either, nor rapes, no serial sexual murderers, no women taking steroids to look more like men, and no children being wrestled into vans to never be seen alive again. All the sexual horror and atrocity our society engenders on a daily basis is symptomatic of how sick our sexual system really is, and how in need of overhaul.

WELL, HERE WE ARE three-quarters of the way through the chapter on sex and we haven't said a word about a guy's dick. His cock. His penis. The organ seems so unimportant in the scheme of things. Lesbians can replace them with sperm banks and a turkey baster.

There is a learned book titled *Christ's Sexuality in Renaissance Art*, with lots of dirty pictures of Jesus naked on the Cross, all of them done hundreds of years ago. I don't think many have him circumcised, and most show him with an abnormally small peepee. Of course he was circumcised, and I'd hope his dick was at least as big as the next man's.

The Gospels seem in accord that Jesus was first stripped naked, and then put on the Cross. But even the fundamentalists seem to want to override the Bible on this point, and show our Lord daintily draped in a short white sarong.

Censored. For decency. To protect our virgin and pure women folk. To protect our innocent children. To not be like the ignorant heathen, the naked savage. The Samoan.

But it ain't working. All the sex crime and sick perversion are symptomatic of the sickness of our Puritanism.

MOST OF WHAT I said about little boys and their mommies applies to little girls and their daddies. Although Freud was wrong about a lot of stuff, he was right about a lot of stuff, too, including the sexuality of girls and boys. Little girls want to see it and feel it. You have to set limits on them, but not by making them feel guilty or afraid of their sexual yearnings. Remember the mother in the bank line? Make it a father on the couch watching TV with six-year-old Felicha. Same set of rules applies.

I learned from my adult women clients that many daughters feel a strange rejection by Daddy when they first grow breasts and hips and commence their monthly bleedings. Daddy disappears into the garage workshop and becomes intent on woodworking and isn't emotionally available to them any more. Daddy gets outraged because his once darling daughter is wearing a sleeveless dress. Daddy becomes morbidly suspicious and accusatory about how his girl spends her times out on dates.

Actually, I think, Daddy is feeling sexually attracted, consciously or unconsciously, by his darling daughter, and if he gets guilty or frightened about these inevitable feelings, they can drive him to be cold, mean, crazy, or all three.

Please remember, gentle reader, that you and I are animals. Not just animals, of course: animals and something more, but, nevertheless, animals. We poop, just like the whale and dung beetle. We need water, just like every other living thing. We need to move. We have senses.

O.K., not just any animal. First, we are mammals: warm-blooded, and the girls get to have wombs and give milk. And second we are Simians (not Canines or Felines). Third we are Great Apes. We share 98.4 percent of our DNA with the chimpanzee: we have more genetically in common with him than he has with our mutual cousin, the gorilla.

And the animal part of us, the chimpanzee-like part of us, plays a part in everything we do, and how we feel: We and the chimp both hunger, thirst, eat, drink, fight, flee, sleep, poop, pee, court, fuck, see, hear, feel, scratch, clown, laugh. The animal-chimpanzee-human list of shared realities goes on.

But here is some terrible news. Animals have no rules against incest.

None at all. True, the alpha male can keep all the young buckaroos at bay; but if a human scientist or animal breeder wants to get Herman the chimp and his mother, or Sheila the chimp and her brother alone in a cage or enclosure during the right time in estrus when the female's in heat, then by God the chimps are going to feel like doing the nasty, and furthermore, are going to do it and feel good about it.

Incest laws are fine. All human cultures have them. The Samoan incest laws were and are every bit as strong as ours. I'm just saying that underneath those very good laws are some natural inclinations that run counter to them, and we need to be aware of that.

I once saw a ten-year-old boy in psychotherapy whose most dramatic presenting symptom was suicidal threat. He told his mother, the school, and eventually me that he was going to kill himself. This symptom emanated from his very deep depression—and remember that depression is often anger turned inward, a condition that suicide takes to the extreme.

The boy was maturing early, and already had a touch of manly muscularity to his body and a smudge of wispy mustache. He lived alone with his divorced mother, a slender blonde given to wearing thin sundresses.

The two fought all the time. Fought hard. Fought long. Both felt constantly injured by the other. They were a miserable couple, although mother put on a brave face.

One day the light dawned for me. They were feeling some underlying attraction. After all, most of my friends in junior high felt free to notice how attractive some of our pals' mothers were, or some of our teachers, just not our own mother. My client and his housemate mother, who had no boyfriends, were feeling something, feeling very guilty about the something they were feeling, and taking that sense of extreme badness out on each other. Not that that was their only problem, but that that was the problem they weren't conscious of, and so it was especially difficult to deal with.

Mother was a fundamentalist Christian. When I told her my views on the situation, she didn't like them at all. In fact, she went into a state of what might be interpreted as furious denial. So I backed off.

But I've offered that same interpretation in a number of other similar family circumstances since then, and I've been happily surprised by how many folks it made instant sense to. They already knew it was going on, but no one had licensed them to think about it out loud. I will only talk about this with a single mom in private, though, and let her work things out.

I can't remember ever seeing a single dad who was living alone with his adolescent daughter. I suppose it happens, but I haven't run across it.

Remember, too, these sorts of psychological or emotional incest issues can also occur in two-parent families.

THERE'S A RESEARCH PROJECT that gets repeated every couple of years or so and always comes out with the same result. The researchers get a large random group of people and ask them a lot of questions, like how old are you, how much school did you complete, how much money do you make, what's your religion, do you own your own home? Just about everything you can think of, including, on a scale of 1 to 10, how happy are you?

Every time they run the answers through the computer they get the same result: single women are the happiest group, followed by married men. Coming in third are married women. Least happy are single men.

Men as a group are just a lot more dependent, both physically and emotionally, than they want to be. And too many men are in denial about their dependence.

In the movies the man who always lives alone comes riding out of the woods on a large horse and brings much-needed and deadly justice to a western town. While he's there, and in between shooting bad guys, he takes a brief timeout to couple in the hay barn with a blonde dressed in gingham who has been wanting him ever so badly since their eyes first met. Then he goes back to the town saloon and shoots the shit out of seven or eight more bad guys, all of whom had their guns trained on him a second before the shooting started. Then he rides out of town and back into the woods, alone.

This image of masculinity, the strong man who needs no one, and who keeps his sexual life limited to gorgeous strangers he's known for just a short while (quite the opposite of how he likely felt toward mommy during his formative years), finds itself expressed in all the James Bond movies and a number of movie heroes make their living playing variations on this theme in everything from science fiction to detective stories.

It is ultimately a sick and unrealistic fantasy, especially to those who are not only entertained by it but live their lives trying to emulate it. With painfully few exceptions, very few movies, or books for that matter, portray passion continued through a marriage. We can find autobiographical mention of it in the poems of e. e. cummings and Tennyson, but who reads poetry these days?

WHICH BRINGS US TO the first scientific discovery in this section, because everything else so far is just reworked Freud and Jung with a little common language and common sense mixed in.

The discovery is PMO. PMO causes a great deal of havoc among both the many men who suffer from it, and the people they encounter, especially the women people.

Symptoms of PMO include irritability, sullen withdrawal, confusion, explosive anger, petulance, and mood swings. PMO also masks itself as overly affable, grinning, concessionary, and completely charming.

PMO causes trouble, is trouble, and until now has gone about creating its mischief and tragedy without being recognized by the population at large.

PMO is not to be confused with its womanly counterpart, PMS, which is actually like PMO in many ways. PMS, or Pre-Menstrual Syndrome, has been working its irritating and destructive effects on both the woman and the man she loves since the dawning of history, but somehow remained invisible until recent years. Now a man knows why his wife treats him like a dog for days at a time, and rather than taking it personally, he chalks it up to the periodic turbulence of her hormones.

I discovered PMO, or Pre Male Orgasm, while observing, not a lab animal exactly, but like a lab animal, an animal under the constraints of human care: in this case a billy goat confined to a farm pen built with stout eight-foot-high fence boards. The pen was, in proportion to this large animal's size, no bigger than a laboratory cage.

It was the thunderous sound of Billy repeatedly crashing his muscular body against those boards, and the loud clattering of the stout gate, that brought my attention to the fiercely troubled animal. When I stood on a table and peered over the top of the fence I saw our hormonally overwrought hero banging furiously, futilely, and unceasingly against his man-made confines.

Something about the level of his rage and anguish, and his smell, resonated with my own animal masculinity. I understood, or felt, his pain. He wasn't mean, or really dangerous, he was just in rut. He had PMO.

Men share this affliction of PMO with gorillas, dogs, and billy goats, but I think men have it worse than the other animals for psychological reasons. Other animals don't have to deal with the images of beautiful and sensual women found in sexual magazines and movies, women with tight skirts and low-cut blouses, plucked eyebrows, and shiny lip gloss; in short, chimpanzees don't need to cope with all the added tricks our own lovely ladies use to get and keep our manly juices flowing.

Plus, the human male knows the girl may open wide on any day, any hour, any moment. All the other dogs can sleep around the barn until the bitch they're attracted to drops her eggs into the uteral basket and sounds the silent siren alarm of pheromone bouquet. This exciting event usually happens on a regular and periodic schedule, often measured in months, and big pups are free to run with the pack and have other fun until it again occurs.

PMO (or in the special case of the fifteen- to twenty-five-year-old man, Testosterone Poisoning) can best be cured or alleviated by a good orgasm. Let's face it, though: social rules and realities often dictate that the orgasm be brought on by the sufferer's own hand.

Every right-thinking man wants a happier solution to this serious, periodic, and lifelong problem, and the best of all solutions is a happy and sacramental marriage.

People who see their mommy and the Virgin Mary as chaste, pure, and sexless are going to have a very tough time enjoying this solution for reasons I've already covered. They are also going to be very angry with me and what I am saying for reasons I've also covered, namely their own self-righteous denial. But actually, no less an authority than the Catholic Church finds both Jesus and his Mother to be sexual beings, just that they remained chaste and celibate for a calling higher than marriage. But they felt, and were, plenty sexual. They both had the urge.

For most of us though, less saintly than Jesus and Mary, marriage is the highest calling. The Church has been around a couple of thousand years and has seven sacraments: Baptism, Confession, Communion, and so on. Marriage is one of the seven.

Being the vice president of Pepsi-Cola or a football hero is not a sacrament. Being Mother of the Year or Grandfather of the Year is not a sacrament. Having $35 billion in your bank account is not a sacrament. But marriage made the cut. Marriage is a sacrament.

Marriage is the best container for this miracle called sex. Although it's all a miracle, isn't it? The fact that you are alive at all, and able to read these words is inexplicable and ultimately grounded in mystery and far beyond the impressive Latin and Greek mumbo-jumbo our media-presented scientists in white coats use to hypnotize us into some sad imitation of certainty. No, folks, we don't really know what the hell is going on, and it's better to know we don't know, at least not in the intellectual sense of knowing. Then we can go on to what works in a realistic way, and that is faith, and hope, and love.

So please think it over, long and deeply, and I believe you'll agree that in the long run of the average lifetime the best of all frameworks for enjoying the gift of Eros, with its vast span of pleasure from gentle rubbings to infinite ecstasy, is that old humble-pie idea of sexual relations called matrimony, tying the knot, putting on the ball and chain, shacking up 'til one of you dies.

I know there are many, many unhappy marriages, and I believe I've suggested some of the common mistakes and fears that feed into dulling our lusting after one another as we become growingly dependent on our wife or hubby and they take on the kind of size and importance that our mothers and fathers once had for us. Perhaps the boy in the bank line is by now running his hands up his wife's skirt, a wife he feels he needs as much as he once needed mommy, and finally enjoying the soft and intoxicating feel of her sweet pussy. And they've been married twenty-five years or more.

Here are a few pointers: First, you are not ready to get married until you have been really happily single for at least a year or two. You have to honestly be able to tell yourself that you are happy and single, and that you would rather be happy and single than unhappily married. When the time comes that you can honestly say that for a year, then you can ask yourself if you would rather be happily married than remain the happy single person you already are.

If the answer is yes, then the time has come to start looking seriously for a spouse, as you are now ready to give up the dating game and all the short-term unhappy-ending romances you've been going through. Some of you will be fifty when this day comes, some eighteen.

You are now looking for a fiancée who, like you, has been happily single a while. None of this "I wasn't happy until I met you."

If you do find this person, and both of you happily single people really want to remain happy, but together, and you like the idea of becoming and staying one flesh (husband, you will have to leave your mother and father and cleave to your wife) then kneel down and thank God, or, at least, count your lucky stars. You can now begin to go beyond sex, wondrous as sex is, and start learning to really make love.

3

God

Oh my God
God of all and everything
Thou art great beyond every thing
and beyond all description
and thou art small and unnoticeable
and invisible beyond any magnifying
and so we call you Alpha and Omega
and you are larger and farther than the star we cannot see
and smaller than the bug that makes us itch but is also
invisible
and you are funny as a parrot
and nobler than the lion you made to delight and frighten us
and you are dark as a lover
that wraps their legs around us
and makes us one with them.

A hard part of talking about God is that so many folks think there isn't any such thing, and I don't blame them, because believing God exists is every bit as far-fetched as believing God doesn't exist. You could get the Harvard debate team debating this subject and both sides could do a wonderful job on either side of the question, and they could go on arguing from here to eternity with neither side really winning or losing if they were at all evenly matched. Because the question can't be resolved logically or rationally.

William Blake, the visionary poet, seemed to see God in a single grain of sand, and I can find proof of God's existence in a dollop of sour cream spread on dark rye bread, or, if pressed, just in the sour cream alone, which would be a little closer to Blake's vision.

But other folks can learn about a star that is so large it's big enough to contain the whole Earth, Sun, and all the other planets in our solar system swinging around each other in full orbit, and so far from us we can't even see it with a telescope; they can learn about such a wonder and still maintain there is no God and that we people are just a pile of chemicals.

Not only is there no dissuading them, but if they are also always patient and kind, and don't puff themselves up, why then they're probably more Godly than I am, even if I have the faith to open Christian bookstores or move mountains.

Really believing God exists is almost always a matter of experience, and a quick change of mind usually occurs only when you are galloping your horse to Damascus and God knocks you out of your saddle and bump bump onto the ground, then chastises you in a loud voice and blinds you for a few days while you mull things over with your well-trained pharisaical intellect.

On a special day many years ago, when we lived in the country on an orchard hill overlooking a wooded creek with a redwood forest standing on the hillside at the back of our property, I had one of those life-shaping experiences, and it involved a boy of seven who also happened to be my youngest son.

On the day I am talking about I was still working on a problem that is now quite dated, the problem of what to answer when someone asked me, "What's happening?"

"What's happening" was a way of saying hello that was new for us White Folks. The Black Folks had been using it for decades or more, but this was the early 1970s, and this piece of black idiom was just beginning to cross over.

It is really such a big question: "What's happening?" It is a cosmic question, a universal question really, because it has no boundaries. It includes the sun and stars, all the oceans, all the electrons, you and all the other people, everything.

And I was answering as best I knew how with, "Nothing much." Or, "Not much."

Which is also a tricky and thought-provoking set of words, if you stop and think long enough about it. I mean, "nothing" means "nothing," doesn't it? And "much" means "much," which is to say a lot of something. So why would you ever put them together, and when you do, what do they mean?

Just to be on the safe side I asked two black friends of mine, one a young man and one an old man, what they answered when someone asked them what's happening, and they both thought about it a while. And the young man answered, "I don't know, I guess I say, 'Nothing much.'" And the old man said, "I don't know, Brother Howard. I guess I say, 'Not much.'"

So although I was still puzzled by the question and not certain of the real answer, I had enough information to get me by for a while. And those were the answers I used, though I never felt entirely easy about them.

Then one day I was walking up the hill on my way to our chicken coop, which stood near our rear property line just in front of a redwood forest, and I was walking through the waist-high grass that grew every year and was dry and golden now because it was just about time for plowing, and I came across my youngest son, just seven years old, and he had tromped down a small circle of grass to sit in, just like a dog will, and he was steadily looking out at the beauty of nature, golden hills of dried grass, budding orchard trees, and the narrow flat valley that held the willow-lined and shimmering creek.

"Hey, Andy," I called out in a cheery voice, "What's happening?"

Andy never moved his head or looked at me; and his expression did not change; his eyes remained fixed on whatever was in front of him and beyond him: all that nature in the sunlight. And he said in even tones, "I don't know."

I kept on walking up the hill, leaving Andrew immersed in what I'm sure was a better world than the one I had in mind, and I knew he had given me the definitive and final answer to the question of "What's happening?"

The answer is "I don't know."

"I don't know" is the ultimate answer for everybody. "I don't know" is at the center of the human condition. All of us are in a constant state of "I don't know," but only the tranquil seven-year-old part of us knows we don't know and accepts the fact. The rest of us are so nervous about that reality, or so anguished by it, that we are willing to kill to defend the lie that we do know.

The women get burned in Salem because we know they are witches. The Catholics and Protestants in Ireland go to great lengths to bomb each other to hell and back because they each know themselves to be right and their brothers to be wrong. Or worse yet they know they aren't brothers, which is an even bigger lie.

We know God exists. Or we know God doesn't exist. We know the Catholic Church is the one religion. Or we know it isn't. We know Buddhism is right. We know Hinduism is right. We know the best politics. We know drugs should be kept illegal. We know the Earth is round. But we used to know the Earth is flat. But now we really know.

Seven-year-olds aren't like that. They still know they don't know. Many of them believe in Santa Claus. Many believe in the tooth fairy. But those beliefs will soon come crashing down. When you were seven and you found out you didn't know, were you terribly surprised about yourself?

Most people, even if they don't believe Jesus resurrected from the dead and is the Son of God, do believe he said some pretty cool things. One of the cool things he said was unless we're like children we can't enter the Kingdom of Heaven.

Part of being like a child is knowing you don't know. It's good to know you don't know. Because it's true you don't. And truth, though sometimes painful, always sets you free. The citizens of the Kingdom of Heaven that Jesus was talking about are always free. It's that kind of perfect Kingdom. The God of Love rules and love is free. But he rules like a shepherd rules. And even the smartest sheep don't know quite what the fuck is going on. He rules like a parent who rules their seven-year-old, and the seven-year-old, if he or she is a happy seven-year-old, knows that Dad and reality are way over their head. Not their heart. Their head.

THERE'S A SELDOM HEARD OF tradition in serious Christianity that has a name that comes from the ancient Greek. The folks in this tradition feel a little indecent about themselves, and what people might think of them, or they would give their belief a simple name, and not a Greek name. The

Greek name is Apophatic, pronounced *a-poe-fat-tic*.

Apophatic is short for *I don't know, and nobody else does*. The apophatics in the church say if you describe God at all, even a little bit, you are instantly rolling in the dust of error. If you say God is infinite, forget about it, you are wrong. If you say God is love, you lose and must go back to Go.

This is because God is so far beyond our comprehension, our ability to intellectualize and put into words, that you are far better off saying nothing about God, thus staying out of the diminishing and erroneous practice of trying to describe him. (An apophatic wouldn't say *him*, or for that matter, *her* or *it*, because that would give one a false sense of thinking they know what's intellectually unknowable.)

These apophatic folks go to Mass on Sunday, and some every day of the week. They say the Lord's Prayer with feeling and conviction, and they love Communion. Many of them are what are usually called Good Catholics, and many can be found living their quiet but illustrious lives in convents and monasteries. Some have written fine books or painted fine paintings. Many have been canonized as saints.

Apophatic Christians most purely practice their conviction about not knowing when they are in a certain form of prayer. The current generic term for that form of prayer is Centering Prayer. The more traditional term is Contemplative Prayer.

Which is to say, prayer that leaves the intellect out, and all words out. Prayer in which the union with God occurs in a wordless act of intention to be with God, and if luck or grace is with you, God has the same intention, and the two of you are one, as lovers are one.

This also goes by the rather spooky term of mysticism, and the poor non-knowing apophatic gets called a mystic. But *childlike lover* is probably a better term, because children don't know either. They are just happy to be with mommy or daddy, feel good, and spend quiet time looking over a beautiful countryside or playing in it and not knowing what's happening but enjoying themselves.

This sort of relationship with God, a relationship beyond ideas and words, has turned a lot of people on. They are happy and stupid at the same time, like a dog when it first sees its master, or a baby when it looks out of the crib and sees its loving father: intense, joyful, and confluent connection; but nothing like what we usually call an idea on anybody's brain.

Sufism, Zen Buddhism, and some other religions have the element of unknowing at or near the center of their practice, and certain Christians are realizing the similarities between their own religion and others and are drawing closer to them in a spirit of fraternity and mutual learning.

Thomas Merton, the Catholic monk and contemplative who died rather mysteriously in Bangkok after giving a talk to a worldwide assemblage of monks from all religions, was a great advocate of the essential oneness found in all people and religions. And he was an apophatic.

Merton is famous in Catholic circles and many other circles of religion. He wrote many books and articles and influenced the heck out of current religious thought. I find it instructive that when he died and they flew his body back to the Kentucky monastery where he had lived his entire adult life as a Trappist monk, a number of his fellow monks refused to attend his funeral because they thought he was an agent of the devil.

It was Merton who during his lifetime had observed that most people say they believe in God but act as if they don't, and most people say they don't believe in the devil but act as if they do. The monks who refused to attend his funeral because they thought their fellow monk was damned were, it seems to me, acting diabolically: which is to say punitively, angrily, and most diabolical of all, despairingly. In their own way they were doing the Devil's work, which is to find as many of us ending up in hell as possible, and those petulant fellow monks of Merton's were believing that Tom had gone below to be roasted in the fire forever. Instead, they should have been kneeling by his graveside praying for his soul. He would have been at theirs, even though he disagreed with them.

Merton seemed to believe we are all saved in the life after this one. He wrote about the more traditional view as well, and coined the remarkable phrase, "the insufferable flippancy of the saved," to indicate a part of what he found wrong with it.

I WAS BAPTIZED A Christian at the age of twenty-seven, which is much closer to the age most people became Christians in the Gospels than the current tradition of sloshing water on young ones before their teeth are in and before they can have any idea at all of who they are or what they believe. Current baptism is more like an inoculation than a conversion, and may account in part for why so many folks who were raised Christian are going elsewhere with their beliefs.

Of course we need that inoculation if we're going to be damned without it; but again, I see little in the Gospels to indicate baptism as the one certain step needed to enter Heaven, or the permanent ticket to stay out of hell, for that matter. Remember, Dante portrayed a great number of well-known people, including a few popes, as eternally damned, heads in the dirt and feet in the air forever, and surely those good Italian boys and girls had been well-baptized on their way to eternal suffering.

Anyway, I was twenty-seven at the time I was baptized and I had my opinions, and I made damn sure I could believe that no one was damned and that everyone was saved and eventually went to Heaven, that I could believe this and still be a Catholic. I got the go-ahead on these beliefs from both a priest at the contemplative Catholic monastery where I was staying and from my godfather and catechism teacher Ernesto Cardenal, who was then thirty-six years old and studying to be a priest, and who had just left a two-year stint in a monastery with Thomas Merton as his novice master. Ernesto did become a priest and has been one now for many years, and we still e-mail or phone once in a while. He lives in Nicaragua.

I SEE IN RETROSPECT that I needed to believe everyone eventually goes to Heaven just to make sure my own sorry skin and soul were saved. I wanted to reasonably hope that even someone who carries as much evil around inside themselves as I do could and would finish up their life doing eternity with a bright and loving God, and all the angels and saints, in an unimaginably joyful Kingdom of Being.

I guess this is where salvation or being saved comes in. I am not going to be able to swim out of the morbid sea of my seven deadly sins, ever. I need a lifeguard to throw me a rope or, better, dive in and rescue me. Lifeguard Jesus. The surer I get that he's doing that for me, the surer I get that he's doing it for everyone.

Let's say you decide to drown and you swim out to do so. If the best lifeguard imaginable knows what you are up to and decides to rescue you, your puny efforts to push him away won't work; no matter how hard you struggle, his good-natured efforts are eventually going to thwart your self-destructive tendencies.

Therefore, if an all-powerful and all-loving God is out to get you to happily join his ongoing afterlife wedding party, eventually he's going to win over your shyness, reservations, and downright refusal. He's got more time to do it in than time itself. More patience than you. And more reserves.

Of course, I don't know if this belief of mine is true any more than you know if your beliefs are true. But, if you're an agnostic and you end up having picnics by a stream with the Virgin Mary, well, don't say I didn't tell you. And if you're a Christian who thinks that just you and a limited number of other wonderfully elite and lucky folks are taking the train to Jordan, I'm warning you, it's going to be better than you've so far imagined. And if you're a Buddhist or a Hindu, well, you won't be that surprised, will you?

FREUD, WHO IS EITHER a saint by now or closing in on becoming one, pointed out that we all have a sex drive that is hardwired into our biology from birth and therefore inescapable, even if we relegate it to our unconscious. He also pointed out that if our parents and community were somewhat sexually twisted at the time we were being raised, we would naturally become somewhat sexually twisted, too.

And that idea, once so radical and scandalous, is presently woven into our popular culture, and most of us are spending some of our adolescent and adult life trying to get sex right after getting it at least somewhat wrong the first time; which is to say, we are trying to find out how best to express that natural sexual drive and manifest it in a way that makes ourselves and others happy and, in the process does no harm to anyone, and perhaps does good for the cosmos at large.

Funny, but what Freud says about sex applies equally to religion. *Because all people are born with a religious or spiritual drive as well as a sexual one.* Every human culture in every place and time obviously needed sex as part of its essential survival equipment. And every human culture in every place and time has had religion and spiritual practice. The earliest archeological digs find human skeletons buried with their food bowls and hunting tools. Rome had its Pantheon. The Bible is filled with stories of the Israelites battling people whose religious beliefs differed from theirs. The anthropologists and archaeologists assure us that religion is a cultural universal. Religion and sex are both part of the human condition, though it is true some people suppress and repress those drives so completely they can no longer feel them consciously.

And just like some sexual practices seem less happy and fulfilling than others (reading pornographic magazines alone in a hotel room, paying a prostitute, raping someone), so it seems to me are certain religious practices (deciding to murder Salmon Rushdie, murdering an abortion doctor, murdering children on the synagogue nursery school playground).

So here is this mysterious and inevitable drive within us, and some of us seem to have learned to make rather the least of it rather than the most of it. We are religious, but we go around with a dour face rather than a happy one, because we are religious and afraid and condemning and punitive rather than religious and trusting and welcoming and forgiving.

Remember, I am not talking about superficial play-acting loving—wearing a mask that looks like love on our face while hiding hate and condemnation in our heart. I am talking about really being loving, with all our heart, all our mind, and all our soul.

And it's hard for me to see how you can think you are making the most of your religious faith, and being as loving as you can be, when you cling to the view that a large proportion of the people living, dead, and yet to be born are on the high or low road to hell, while you have the airline ticket into Heaven. How could you believe in a God so limited, sorry, impotent, so much a failure in His own hopes and dreams? Doesn't the Bible say it is God's will that all souls will be saved? Or do you believe, along with Woody Allen, that God is an underachiever?

Or perhaps you are a Buddhist, either by birth or conversion. I remember that when I walked from the little pueblo church where I had just been baptized, and got back to the monastery where I was staying as a guest, I was greeted at the monastery entrance by a simple campesino Benedictine monk who tearfully embraced me and told me that although all roads led to God, I had chosen the best one. But have I really? The Buddhist probably thinks not, if he thinks in those terms at all.

Most Buddhists believe that everyone eventually reaches enlightenment or Buddahood, partly through reincarnation. If you don't get it right this lifetime, don't worry, you'll be back and will have another shot at it, and so on, until you get it right.

Buddhism lays out the practices for getting it right, but be careful, if you stray too far from those practices, your next lifetime might be as a tarantula. Not hell exactly, not a punishment, just a consequence of straying from a path that, in a way, although at times pleasant and happy-making, is also arduous, straight, and narrow.

If the Buddhists are more in touch with the truth than the Christians, and they may well be, then I may come back next time as a Baptist church lady or a Siamese fighting fish. And remember that I have reason to believe I already have had badly-ending lives as both a nineteenth-century French cavalry officer and a twentieth-century large male gopher.

That is part of why I prefer Christianity. I'm growingly afraid that I'll never get it right during any one lifetime and that I need someone to take care of me, rather than trying to get into heaven by my own industry and discipline.

I believe that when I die again for the umpteenth time and the Buddha smiles and compassionately tells me I've got to hop on the circle once more for another go at it, I'll profess my faith that the famous Jew who died on the cross is picking up my tab at his never-ending celestial celebration. He's the paying host. I'm the unworthy guest. I'm stepping off the long, karmic merry-go-round and entering the final promised land.

First stop is his bathhouse. Next, step into some new and radiant garments he provides, and then mingle and dance with him and the other invitees to his vast wedding celebration. Music by Charlie Parker and the Celestial Choir. Music by Beethoven. Or Gamalon. Or African drums. It's Celebration Time. You all come.

The staff at *TIME* magazine has to work hard at the end of every year to decide who the most newsworthy person was. Then they print one of their weekly editions with a cover story titled "Person of the Year." Then they get letters from readers telling them they picked the wrong person.

If we tried to pick "Person of the Creation" instead of "Person of the Year," I think the choice would boil down to Jesus or Buddha, though I suppose there are still a few folks out there who would pick someone like Johannes Gutenberg or Ronald Reagan.

I think the chances that we can scientifically prove that both Jesus and Buddha were actually born and had real lives, like we are having, is about zero, especially for Jesus. But even if Jesus is a purely fictional character, like Paul Bunyan or Harvey the Rabbit, it is still a showdown title fight between him and Buddha for most important person in the history of history. And personally I believe Jesus did and does live.

Please forgive me, Mohammed. You are very important, I know. Very very important, and so are your millions of followers (three times the number of Buddhists). For the purposes of this book only, my panel of judges has excused you. Your followers may write me. But private assassination attempts or state proclamations calling for my murder are humbly discouraged.

Buddha was born into a royal family and was raised a protected and pampered aristocrat. Even though he had everything that money and privilege could offer, he felt deeply unsatisfied and left the comforts of his palace to make a long, arduous, and adventuresome search for—he wasn't sure exactly what, but whatever it was would deliver him from the pain of all human suffering. He tried various social roles and excitements but all left him rather empty, frustrated, and vaguely unsatisfied.

When he finally found what he wanted, it had been inside him all along. Let's call it enlightenment, which is sort of the extreme opposite of feeling or being heavy. He found enlightenment, release from all suffering, oneness with everything, while he sat under a Bo tree.

For the next forty-five years his main job was gathering disciples and telling anyone who was interested in knowing just how to do what he did and to get where he got. In that way, Buddhism is rather scientific. Follow the basic directions, and you'll get the same results every time.

A lot of people follow, and a lot of people now long dead have followed Buddha's road map, cookbook, experiment, call it what you will. And they feel better, and they are better, and they make and have made the world a better place. All this in very large numbers. Millions and millions and millions. And that's why the Buddha is so important in this sorry-ass world of ours. He's on the side of good and he's making the cosmos a better, happier place.

Oh yes, and because he was born in India he had dark skin, black hair, and dark eyes, just like Jesus and Mohammed.

JESUS, ON THE OTHER hand, was born into a carpenter's family. No palace, but, hey, it's a living. He didn't go searching for enlightenment on his own tack; it was handed to him from the get-go. He was aces up from the start.

As a young man his dad gave him not a fancy sports car or assorted concubines, but a supercharge from the Holy Spirit. This happened down by the river when his cousin John poured water on his head.

Now he had everything. He was either close to or had surpassed the place Buddha had spent so much of his life looking and working hard for. Then he gets a group of a guys and gals together and they go out telling folks about how good God can get, God being Jesus's very own daddy. But this phase lasts only three years, one-fifteenth of the time Buddha spent stumping.

Some of the people Jesus tells love the news. Others get mad as hell: the conservative far-right fundamentalist Jews, a powerful faction (just like the conservative far-right fundamentalists are in Christianity today), don't like him picking wheat on the Sabbath, don't like him boiling their voluminous, precious, and detailed laws into two koan-like admonitions about love, and don't like him getting into disrespectful and verbally victorious confrontations with certain members of the priestly class.

And the Romans, who occupy the country militarily while extracting large amounts of wealth from the Jews through taxes, and who have the cooperation of the country's puppet rulers during this extortion, don't like the prospect of their new world order money-making machine being rocked or busted.

So, for shooting his mouth off once too often, offending the wrong people, and breaking a number of religious and political rules, he gets arrested and tried and sentenced for a capital crime and is executed. All very legal, according to the Roman system, and there is never an appeal or mistrial.

But at the point of his mortal death, Jesus does not immediately leave his disciples behind to spread the word. No. He gets up out of the grave, cooks fish by the seaside, and talks some more to those who love him. He even lets Doubting Thomas stick a finger in the lance wound just to make everyone certain he had resurrected.

Same Jesus, but with an upgraded body. One that can't die. This time he doesn't go around risking offending someone. Only those who believe can see him.

Then, up into Heaven to join with whoever is there celebrating.

SOME OF THE SIMILARITIES between these two contenders for Man of the Creation are pretty obvious. Both have already received billions of votes for glorious leader, and their tallies continue to grow. They both gave a set of rules and principles about how to lead a good life, with the grand payoff being a possible trip to Heaven, or, in Buddha's case, Nirvana or, better yet, Buddahood. Both are men who, although they never salted away a billion dollars, invented the airplane, or headed a political state that eventually conquered Eurasia, are nevertheless top contenders for the title of goodest guy who ever walked this dusty and rapidly becoming asphalt Earth of ours.

Isn't it wonderful that two of the most influential people in history are also the two goodest people in history?

But there are differences, too.

Notice that one had to work very hard to reach his enlightenment and goodness, and that's Buddha.

But for Jesus, the fix was in from the start and he was already top gun the day he was born. The Virgin Birth, the brains he used to astound the rabbis in the temple, the infusion of the Holy Spirit when John baptized him, his own foreknowledge of his coming death and resurrection, those were all gifts.

So one guy, Buddha, was born into material fortune, but had to work like hell for his spiritual abundance, his wisdom, his enlightenment, his virtue.

He was the self-made man. He was also for the most part non-contentious and died in his eighties from eating some contaminated pork.

And the other guy, Jesus, who was born in a manger, inherited his Father's Godhead right away and without apparent effort. It was in the cards he was dealt. He couldn't lose. He was going to get there (he was already there), and get there in style. And what a style. He was the God-made man.

This guy, at least before his resurrection, was often quite contentious, and was legally murdered by some of the powerful people who hated the forms of his contention.

O.K. I'VE MADE MY choice. I'm voting for Jesus. But I want Buddha and Mohammed in the cabinet.

I'm voting for Jesus because his life, although he didn't liberate South Africa or invent the cure for polio, brings about universal salvation, which is to say that because of him everyone eventually goes to Heaven and stays there forever, which is far longer than the grisly or glorious time we spend on Earth, even if we live past a hundred, or recycle through for ten thousand different incarnations. (There are schools of Buddhist practice that believe in the eventual liberation of all sentient beings from suffering, followed by further eventual liberation for all into Buddhahood. So here, too, the goal can be construed as universal salvation. But the Buddhist way sounds like it takes too many lifetimes for me, is too hard for me, doesn't factor in grace enough for me, and I'm not sure I'd get to visit with my mother or meet my old friends when I get there.)

And when this whole world as we know it is over, destroyed by the sun extinguishing, or by a giant meteorite, or by too many mega-neutron bombs bursting in air at the same moment, or by the gradually cancerous effect that humanity is having on the environment, or by some other manifestation of the too-often unbridled evil that humanity seems capable of manifesting in any given century, when it's finally over and it's been done through some act of nature or we ourselves have done it, or God does it like some referee ending a contest where the loser is too badly beaten to go on, then Jesus will step in and rescue all the dead men walking, and all the lost souls drowning.

The gentle and learned Catholic theologians who deal with this question are at times hesitant to accept universal salvation as an article of faith because they find it may contradict the essential nature of human freedom. But I say, give a seven-year-old an absolutely free choice between a pile of dog poo and an ice cream cone, and he'll take the ice cream cone every time, especially if he's already tasted the poopoo.

Now that I've said this many of the folks who disagree with me can run to the Bible and find something in there to show you that there are at least quite a few people currently roasting in Hell now, and quite a few more on their way. And they will say that those suffering people are going to stay there from now on, just roasting and gnashing their teeth, and there's no way out for them, and this is all part of God's wonderful plan.

They are going to find passages in the Bible to support this sad and not totally good news view, and they have lots and lots of company to share their opinion. I have one friend who was told in seventh grade (sixty years or so ago) by a Sunday School teacher that her little Buddhist buddy, who attended a local Buddhist temple, would have to say good-bye to my friend on Judgment Day and then spend eternity in the furnace 'cause she just didn't know Jesus.

My friend left the Christian Church in response to the Sunday School teacher's theology, so I suppose the Sunday School teacher believes my friend is going to Hell, too, even though I can vouch for my friend not being all bad. I wish she would rejoin the church, though, for her own welfare and because we could use her.

FOR A NUMBER OF years I belonged to a group called Christians in Commerce. It's basically a guy group, though the wives are invited to the socials and have their own auxiliary. The guys meet every Wednesday morning for breakfast, prayer, fellowship, and Christian education. They call themselves Christians in Commerce because the members are men who are out in the work world running auto stores and lumberyards, delivering babies, trying legal cases, basically being guys in the marketplace who are trying to work their trades in a Christian way.

The headquarters in Saint Louis prints a monthly newsletter that goes out to local chapters. During the weekly breakfast meetings they read whatever short Biblical passage the newsletter has designated for the week, and then whoever is leading the group that day discusses the meaning of that passage.

One morning the passage was a speech Jesus makes in the Gospel of John, and the passage runs about thirty lines and ends with Jesus saying, "And I, if I be lifted up from the Earth, will draw all men unto me."

Boy oh boy was I happy they were going to discuss this passage, because Christians in Commerce as an official group not only believes there's a Hell, they believe tons of people are being eternally transformed into blackened and agonized toasted marshmallows there. I wondered how the discussion leader, a lawyer and an old friend of mine, was going to handle those words of Jesus, "And I, if I be lifted up from the Earth, will draw all men unto me."

Well, my friend, whose name is Calvin, carefully read, talked about, pondered and analyzed the first twenty-eight lines in the speech, and then he just stopped before talking about the last two lines in front of him. He never mentioned the equally sacred words of Jesus, "And I, if I be lifted up from the Earth, will draw all men unto me." And this was odd as hell, because whoever the weekly leader was, they always covered every line in a particular week's Christians in Commerce Biblical passage.

There were about forty men at the meeting, maybe more. My friend led us in a group discussion about the passage after he had concluded his solo explication, and many of the men gave their input. But no one mentioned or even indirectly alluded to the words, "And I, if I be lifted up from the Earth, will draw all men unto me."

It was kind of like in the story of the Emperor's New Clothes. Everyone acted like they didn't see what was smack dab in front of them. Why didn't I blow the whistle on this game? I wasn't child enough.

Do you remember at the start of this section I said the Harvard debate team could argue all the way to eternity over whether God exists or not? Well, they could take just as long arguing over the question of whether, if he does exist, then does he shepherd everyone into Heaven eventually. I just wanted to mention how Calvin behaved at the Christians in Commerce meeting to point out that sometimes the people in favor of keeping Hell alive and tormenting various souls can throw out or disregard evidence opposed to their position, even though they may be doing it unconsciously.

So I will briefly argue in favor of the belief that God's overwhelming and all-conquering mercy eventually will carry us all into his loving promised land. As an old man used to say to me during the days I was young, "When I die, it's not God's justice I want. I don't want his justice at all. Just his mercy. I just want his mercy." The old man then would go on to say, "I'd be very glad and grateful to start out in the humblest and tiniest and lowest corner of purgatory. Just to have the tiniest place there." His name was Costello, and he was an Irish Catholic who never got overtly angry but was known to stay silent for days at a time when his patience had been sorely tried.

I will argue for the reality of Universal Salvation, fully understanding there is much evidence on the opposing side. I leave you and others to devote your energies to measuring that evidence. I have done it enough. After all, I don't really know. You don't really know. It's ultimately a mystery. I'm just seeking the Kingdom and hoping, for God's sake and my own, that I am right.

To KEEP THIS AS simple as I can, and to work at becoming as good a Jewish lawyer as possible, I'm going to limit my appeal for the currently damned people to four pieces of evidence, all from the words of Jesus as found in the Gospels.

First piece of evidence is the Lord's Prayer, your honor.

Second piece of evidence is the parable of the unforgiving debtor, your honor.

Third piece of evidence are the words of Jesus on the Cross, your honor.

Fourth piece of evidence is the parable of the vineyard workers' wages, your honor.

FIRST PIECE OF EVIDENCE:

Jesus, or God as he is also known, gave us explicit instructions on how to pray. He said don't babble and use a bunch of words, because our Father knows what we need before we ask him anyway. And right after he said this to us he gave us a very short prayer called the Lord's Prayer:

Our Father, who art in heaven
hallowed be thy name.

Thy kingdom come.
Thy will be done on earth as it is in Heaven.
Give us this day our daily bread,
and forgive us our trespasses
as we forgive those who trespass against us.
And lead us not into temptation, but deliver us from evil.

There are two versions of this prayer in the Bible. One leaves out the phrases "Thy will be done on earth as it is in heaven," and "deliver us from evil," or, in some translations, "save us from the Evil One."

But it's the longer, more complete one that we commonly use, perhaps going against the spirit of his advice to keep it as brief as possible.

No big deal. The longer Lord's Prayer is only fifty-nine words, shorter than an ad for a life insurance policy and easier to memorize. The shorter Lord's Prayer is forty-two words, at least in my translation of the Bible.

So, this is God speaking, and we figure if he's only going to use fifty-nine words in his prayer each word must count. In both prayers the words are mostly about how God is and what we want him to do for us: God, You are in Heaven. God, your name is holy. God give us our bread today. God, don't lead us into temptation. God, forgive us our sins. God, deliver us from evil and the Evil One. God, don't put us to the test.

There is only one thing in the Lord's prayer that we ourselves are clearly supposed to do rather than begging God to do it for us, and that is forgive. "Forgive us our sins *as we forgive those who sin against us.*" That's all we have to do. Aside from that, we ask God to do everything.

The Lord cut seventeen words and a few ideas out of one of his two short exemplary prayers, but he left the part about our forgiving others in both of them. He must think our forgiving others is very important, maybe even essential. Wouldn't you agree?

SECOND PIECE OF EVIDENCE:

In the parable of the unforgiving debtor, Jesus tells the story of a man who owed his king around seventy million dollars, and the king was getting ready to throw the guy into some lousy prison because he couldn't pay.

But the guy begs for forgiveness so pitifully that the king cancels his debt entirely and lets him go free.

Then the freed man bumps into someone who owes him only a few hundred dollars and he grabs him by the throat and says either pay up now or I'll have you thrown into the prison. And when the guy can't pay, he actually does have him put away in some dark hole.

When the king hears of this he has the first debtor brought before him and angrily tells him he had no business being unforgiving when he had himself been forgiven so much.

Then the king has the first guy, the unforgiving debtor "handed over to the torturers 'til he should pay all his debt."

And Jesus adds, "and that is how my heavenly Father will deal with you unless you each forgive your brother from your heart."

What do you make of this parable? After all, it starts out with Jesus saying, "And so the Kingdom of Heaven may be compared to a king who decided to settle his accounts with his servants."

This is Heaven and Hell we are talking about, and how to stay out of one and get into the other.

I identify with the unforgiving debtor, someone who owes God the King so much that I can never adequately repay him. He's given me my life, and at present, my wife, my happy marriage, my lovable career, my children and grandchildren, my health, the air I breathe, and the hope I have in eternity. I, in return, remain in large measure a sinner. There is no way I can repay my debt. All I can do is ask God to forgive me. If God doesn't forgive me, I'm going to prison.

If I want to stay out of prison—Hell, that is—and remain a free citizen of the Kingdom of Heaven (remember the parable), I have to forgive everyone else, and keep on forgiving. Forgive all my debtors for the injuries they've inflicted on me, forgive myself for all the harm I've done to others and myself, even forgive God for any grudges I'm holding against him, however unjustified.

THIRD PIECE OF EVIDENCE:

Most of us are fascinated with last words, the last words someone says before they die. There are books called Famous Last Words, and you can read what someone famous said on the battlefield or their deathbed and then never said anything again because after a lifetime of talking they stopped talking altogether and either extinguished or moved on to the next plane, depending on how you think about it.

Everyone knows Jesus was a great talker, and that he talked and talked and talked, and some people loved what he said and others decided to kill him for what he said, and people by the thousands would listen to him talk, stay all day and have lunch in the open air, and this was before the days of the loudspeaker system or a giant stadium video screen.

On top of this he was alleged to be the son of God, so we know he is going to speak some very important last words. And he spoke all of those last words from the cross he was crucified and killed on, with lots of folks around, including his mother and disciples to hear him, and his last words got written down in four books called the Gospels.

Those words are referred to as the Seven Last Words, Joseph Haydn wrote an oratorio about them, and all things considered you know that each of them must have been very important. One is, "I'm thirsty." That was probably an early one. Another is, "Father, into thy hands I commend my spirit." Probably one of his last, last words. Then there is one which is different from the others, because it is the only one where he is telling God to do something, and that is, "Forgive them, Father, because they don't know what they are doing."

And because that different one, the one that goes, "Forgive them Father, for they know not what they do," is one of the Seven Last Words, spoken from the cross by God to God at what may be the most important moment in human history, I think we should give it special attention.

The key question is who did Jesus mean by "*them*" when he said, "Forgive them."

Well, let's look at how this fellow usually used words. Like when he said, "Let him who has not sinned cast the first stone." Did he mean just that group of stoners who had gathered to kill the adulteress? Or did he mean other Pharisees as well, for example, all the ones in Israel at the time? Or did he mean everyone, everywhere, all the time? The usual view, and the commonsense view, is that he meant everyone, everywhere, all the time. And that includes you and me, sisters and brothers.

Or when he said "Love your neighbor as yourself," did he mean just one neighbor? (He didn't say "*neighbors*," you know). Or did he mean just the neighbors on either side of your house? Or did he mean the ones across the street as well? How about the ones down the block?

Or did he mean everyone, everywhere, all the time?

Jesus generally used words in a very inclusive way. His language was vast and far-reaching, universal, just as God is.

When he said, "Forgive them, Father, for they don't know what they are doing," did he just mean the Jews and Romans who had trespassed against him? Or did he mean everyone, everywhere, all the time?

It would be consistent with the way he usually talked for him to have meant everyone, everywhere, all the time when he was dying and told God the Father to forgive "them" for they don't know what they are doing. Giving reality the benefit of the doubt, that's just what he was saying.

And since he himself was God, and the Word of God, he was telling us all what God was doing, letting us in on the secret when he knew everyone was listening. The secret is he saved us all on the cross: everyone, everywhere, all the time. And God forgives us all, everyone, everywhere, all the time, even the people you especially hate or dislike, the ones you haven't forgiven and the ones you want in hell, you unforgiving debtor, you.

Let those who have ears, hear.

Fourth Piece of Evidence:

Jesus tells the parable of the laborers in the vineyard and again begins with the relevant words, "The Kingdom of Heaven is like . . ."

In this story, a landowner starts hiring day workers at the break of dawn and gets them hustling away in his vineyard, but before they start they've agreed to their daily wage.

A few hours later he hires some more guys who are standing around.

A few hours later he does the same thing with some new guys.

Finally, with just an hour to go before quitting time, he hires the last bunch.

When the workday is over he starts paying the crew off, and he starts with paying the guys who had been working for only the last hour and he ends with paying the guys who have been working the whole day, and he pays them all exactly the same amount.

The men who had been working since daybreak start grumbling because they've worked so much longer and are still getting the same payoff as the guys who showed up just a little before dark.

And the owner of the vineyard says, first, that they got the pay they signed up for, and second, "Why should you be envious because I am generous?"

This story obviously has something to do with time and what we do during it. Like, I've been a Christian since I was twenty-seven so I joined the vineyard work later than the guy who was born into Christianity. And a friend of mine became a Christian when she was fifty-three, so I've been sweating the job longer than her.

Which reminds me of the first time I was high on LSD and I looked at my watch, and then three or four hours went by, and I looked again, and only twenty seconds had actually elapsed, but because of my psychological state the twenty seconds had seemed like three or four hours and that's what God, who can do anything he damn well pleases, can do with your sense of time. Which means if you suddenly drop dead from a bullet or a burst blood vessel in your brain, God and all the angels and saints can spend three or four thousand years showing you the difference between eternity in Hell or eternity in Heaven, and you'd be like the kid deciding between poopoo and ice cream, and what do you suppose you'd choose, and all this could happen in the instant it took you to hit the floor, and in that instant God could have you working in the vineyard, maybe running errands for the angels for a few centuries, and those of us who chose Heaven early on in life had better not grumble at either your good fortune or at God's generosity.

Besides, I'd rather spend as much of my daylight hours working in the vineyard as possible; it's fun, and there's good company.

AND THAT CONCLUDES THE evidence in appeal and defense of the currently damned, your honor.

Damned in your view, your honor, but not in mine. And not in the view of many, your honor, for there are many like me who believe everyone goes to Heaven. That means everyone goes eventually: me, you, Adolph Hitler, Judas Iscariot, Carrie Nation, the whole bunch. All eventually blessed, the long and the short and the tall.

That the score is God: Everyone; Devil: Zero.

That the game was won when Christ's spirit soared over the crossbar.

Of course, History goes on after the crucifixion, so as not to make a mockery of History before he arrived. He's the Man of the Creation, the guy who influenced History most, but he didn't do away with History altogether. He just leavened it, like yeast leavens a large lump of otherwise lifeless dough. And the dough rises slowly.

For example, most Christian nations have given up the death penalty altogether. And though America has regressed to using the death penalty again, no one draws and quarters the criminal anymore like they once did, or cuts out the criminal's heart and holds it beating before his startled eyes. Not even in America.

And medicine is now available to everyone who lives in an industrialized Christian nation, except of course in America.

And far fewer people in industrialized Christian nations go homeless and hungry, which is to say the poor are being taken better care of than before, except currently that is not the case in America, which is mass producing poor with the same efficiency it once produced automobiles.

And fewer people are mercilessly sentenced to years in prison for petty crimes like stealing a small loaf of bread or owing someone money, except in America where, with marijuana laws and three-strike laws, imprisonment is a growth industry.

So if we look at History since the day Christ died on the cross we could say that people as a group are getting steadily kinder and more considerate of others and fewer people are being left to rot on the streets or in prison than they once did in Christian countries, except perhaps currently in America.

And also certain people who have tried to follow Jesus after he died and rose from the dead have made spectacular differences in the world. Let's take just three famous ones: Joan of Arc, Martin Luther King, and Mother Teresa.

Have you heard of the Pulitzer Prize-winning historian, Barbara Tuchman? She's an atheist but she wrote a good book called *A Distant Mirror* that talks about a war between France and England that lasted a hundred years, killed and maimed too many people, and almost bankrupted both countries because both were forever in a "defense" mode, and there was just no way of ending it in sight, and then along came a Christian teenage girl named Joan of Arc, and Barbara Tuchman, who is an atheist, remember, says Joan ended it, doing so for God's sake, which to Barbara Tuchman was a delusion, but ending it nevertheless.

A bloody miracle documented by an atheist that changed History for the better by someone who was following Christ. Someone the Catholic Church burned at the stake and killed as a heretic, which meant they believed she was going straight to hell in a fiery handbasket, but then later the Church changed its mind and made Joan of Arc a saint.

And Martin Luther King, a very imperfect man and an adulterer, who said there was such a thing as "unearned suffering," thus proving himself to be no Karma-bound Buddhist, and he was referring to all the black folk who had been born into Jim Crow-suffering, and also to the Original Unearned Suffering Sufferer, the guy he followed, Jesus Christ, who, like many black men whom Martin Luther King knew or knew of, had also had the shit beaten out of him by government cops and sent to death row in a prejudiced but perfectly legal trial.

So Martin Luther King broke some of the stupid and unjust laws of his day, just like Jesus did, and following Jesus he made History a better place to live in, more in accord with something like Saint Paul once said, "Know you not that there is neither White Man nor Black Man but we are all one in Jesus Christ?" And like Jesus and Joan of Arc he paid the price for disagreeing with and vanquishing the diabolic status quo, paid for it with his life.

Mother Teresa is a high school teacher who later became a principal and then followed what she thought was a call from Jesus, followed the call into the hellholes of Calcutta, and to a significant degree winnowed them, and then went round the world with her other followers of Jesus making History a better place, especially for the poorest of the poor.

And that's just three of such people but there are so many more, Damien the Leper, Peter Claver, Martin de Porres, Vincent de Paul, and all the folks no one has heard of, all the fools who tried to imitate Jesus and couldn't come close except perhaps in some comic way, but they were better, and History was better, because they tried.

THIS MAN JESUS, WHO giving him the benefit of the doubt was also God, said, "I haven't come to change the law one jot or one tittle," and on another occasion said to his old pal Peter, "On this rock I will build my church" and, "I will give you the keys of the Kingdom of Heaven: whatever you bind on Earth will be bound in Heaven; whatever you loose on earth will be loosed in Heaven." And so with these words in mind, and with everything else I've said in mind, I write the following open letters to the Pope:

Dear Holy Father Pope Francis,

Fifteen years ago I wrote the letter you'll see below. I wrote it to Pope John Paul II, but my book was refused publication by a number of publishers and for a long while it remained unpublished.

Then Pope John Paul II died, and Pope Benedict XVI replaced him; yet the following letter seemed to fit Pope Benedict, too.

(I believe it was Benedict who changed the wording of the mass from consecrated wine being, "given up for all," to merely being "given up for many." Pope Benedict may have been less awestruck, less thrilled, than the pope who decided Christ's blood had been shed for all, and not merely for many.)

Still, I'm happy this letter may still fit for you, just not as well as it fit your two immediate predecessors.

Nor does it fit Pope John XXIII quite as well either. He once wrote that our Catholic Church wasn't to be seen or treated as a museum, but rather as a garden.

I know all four of you popes are brothers, but perhaps you and John XXIII are the closer brothers.

That said, here is the letter.

I hope we can talk about the letter, and perhaps the book, sometime.

Your brother in Christ Jesus,

Jose Howard

Dear Holy Father,

I hope this letter finds you happy and well and with your customary infallibility in matters of faith and morals.

The simple fact that you go by the title of Holy Father, as is customary in our beloved Catholic church, indicates your willingness to depart from a strict fundamentalist interpretation of the Biblical Gospels in which Jesus admonishes us to "Call no man your Father. You have one Father and he is your Father in Heaven."

But you, Holy Father, and indeed all of our Catholic priests and parishioners, have somehow seen fit to ignore this simple admonition of Jesus, and I know you have many and perhaps subtle reasons for doing so.

I went to see one of your predecessors once when he came to California and many thousands of us gathered on the hillside and he spoke during the Mass he celebrated and during the Mass I heard him say with the rest of us that "I have sinned exceedingly in thought word and deed, in what I have done and in what I have failed to do," and then he asked God for mercy.

And just before he ate the body and drank the blood of Jesus he said with the rest of us, "Lord I am not worthy that you should enter my body, but only say the word and I shall be healed."

And I believe you say these words we all heard your predecessor say that foggy but sunlit morning at least once every day, and I know that no member of the Catholic Church can omit saying and believing those same words when he or she attends Mass. That neither you nor I, nor any member of the Church, however saintly, can go to Mass and omit those words, thinking that today I haven't sinned exceedingly so I needn't say those words, or today I am worthy that God should enter my body so I needn't say those words.

And so I have an idea for you, Holy Father, a good idea I think, and one that our Lord would approve of, and that is to use your power of binding and loosing things on earth and knowing they are then bound and loosed in Heaven and declare that when Jesus suffered and died on the Cross he saved everybody without exception, which is to say that through him every person that dies eventually goes to Heaven.

After all, on the day you die, if you can still talk and receive communion you will still be declaring yourself a sinner and unworthy for God to enter your *body, so if it is by God's grace and mercy that you bypass the gates of Hell, why not everybody?*

*For in Mass we also always say the words, "This is my blood, given up for you and for **all men** so that sins may be forgiven." (Emphasis mine, Holy Father).*

Jesus told us he didn't come to change the law one jot or one tittle, but the law allows itself to change legally, so in that respect change is part of the law, so that now in many countries people do not go to prison for stealing a small loaf of bread, as they once did, because laws change and become less unendurable, less like the unendurable burdens that Jesus accused the lawyers of piling on people's backs, and this is in part because of the leavening effect, the lightening and rising, that his life has had on all of History, and on the human condition.

Since you fervently hope and pray that he has forgiven you your exceeding debts, Holy Father, why not forgive your fellow sufferers their debts, including the debt of being atheists or unrepentant sinners, and pass a law on earth that will be loosed in Heaven and gives us all a ticket into the Loving God's eternal presence. The long and the short and the tall, Holy Father. As you judge, so shall you be judged, Holy Father. Universal Salvation, Holy Father.

And since this may be my last letter to you, I have a further and far less important request, and I make this request from the point of view of a Jewish Catholic, which is a point of view that is at least in some ways different than an Irish Catholic's, an Italian Catholic's, a Polish Catholic's, and so on.

In the church I attend there is a life-size crucifix above the altar, and a life-size body of Jesus there for all to see, and from the look of this thing you would never know the event ever actually happened in real life because his skin is so white that he could never have been out in the sun day after day, and his skin is so free of bruises and wounds that you'd never know he'd been beaten up by the government cop goons, and he has a dainty sarong draped around his loins so you'd never know he'd been stripped naked before being mounted up there and that in real life his circumcised penis had been showing.

In short, people aren't confronted with the reality that complete and perfect Divine Love walked among us in brown skin and we responded with hatred and brutality.

And also, Holy Father, on that plaster crucifix in my church, Jesus doesn't look the least bit Jewish. If anything he looks English. And that, too, denies historical reality, and makes it easier for people to go into denial about what really happened 2,000 years ago, and where it happened, and with whom it happened. As you know, Holy Father, many people hate anyone Jewish and they are up to killing six million Jews at one time and have done so in the last one hundred years. I think it would ultimately help History, and further leaven it, if you encouraged people to portray Jesus as the Jew he was, and to set Italian, Irish, Polish, and other Catholics with the daunting and soul-healing task of finally loving those they have long identified as their enemy.

And lastly, Holy Father, there is a representation of the Last Supper on display in my city, and all the figures are rendered in wax, as realistic as those in Madame Tussaud's wax museum, and everyone at the table—Jesus, John, Peter, and all the disciples—looks English, with blond or light brown hair and blue eyes and fair skin, and what we like to call even features.

Everyone, that is, except Judas, who looks dark and swarthy, with high cheekbones and an eagle's beak nose—a correct, though somewhat mean and crafty, representation of what Jews of that time may have looked like; but he's the only historically accurate-looking figure there. It's as if you had a mock-up of the life of Confucius and everyone including Confucius looked straight out of Africa instead of straight out of China. That would be false, misleading, and ultimately confusing, and a departure from historical truth.

So perhaps you could talk to some of your people, especially the artists, to set about righting these other wrongs, and thus help make the world a better and more truthful place.

Your brother in Christ and in the interest of truth,
José Howard

AND SO WE COME rather near to the end of Chapter 3, the chapter on God, whoever that is, and if there is a God at all. And for those who do believe, I like the spirit and words of the campesino monk Hermano Mateo, who greeted me at the gate of the monastery named Nuestra Señora de la Resurreccion, which rested in the country hills a short way from the pueblito Santa Maria, the pueblito where I had just been baptized. He said that all roads lead to God, but that I had chosen the best one.

The final end is the same for all of us, but some means are more fun and exciting than others. Just ask Martin Luther King, Joan of Arc, or Mother Teresa.

And if this final end, this Omega, exists, and if he is omnipresent, then he spans the entire universe which as we now know is very large, large beyond our seeing with instruments and far beyond seeing with the naked eye we were born with. And very small, too, this Alpha, made up of atoms that are made up of electrons and neutrons, that are in turn made up of things smaller yet, until it all gets so small that the whole idea of matter fuses with the whole idea of energy and we discover that we and everything else material are made up of something where matter and energy simply become one, and there are no spaces in between; the whole cosmos is just one vast interrelated garment of light-matter or matter-light. We as yet have no word for the oneness that the post-Newtonian, post-Einsteinian physicists have discovered. But the oneness is everywhere and we are part of it.

Though if God is everywhere then, it still appears he spreads himself thinner in some places than others. Like when you look out from a tall building at Orange County, California, on a smoggy day, it seems God has spread himself thinner there.

But on the other hand, it seems God concentrates and intensifies his presence in other places, and I visited two such places in one day, and spent hours in both of them.

It was a Saturday and at ten in the morning that I was at the local synagogue attending the Bar Mitzvah of a friend's son, a Bar Mitzvah being the ceremony celebrating a boy's entrance into the Jewish religion as a fully adult member. A young Jew waits until age thirteen for this privilege, and must study Judaism, the Hebrew language, and especially the Torah, the first five books of the Bible, books like Genesis, Exodus, Deuteronomy, the same ones all Christians revere.

When he has studied enough, he gets up before a temple full of people like me who were invited for the event and reads from the Torah and gives a speech, and people close to him, like mom and dad, grandma and grandpa take part in the celebration, there is music and singing, and the whole thing lasted three hours which seemed long to me, but it was very moving.

I don't go to temple very often anymore, usually just for a friend's son's

Bar Mitzvah, or a friend's funeral, but such events do, among other things, keep my memories of religious Judaism more current.

Then a few hours after the Bar Mitzvah I went to Mass at our local Catholic church, because I try to go to Mass once a week, and if you go late Saturday afternoon they call that a Vigil Mass which means you needn't go to Mass on Sunday and can sleep in and watch football instead. God is merciful.

And both the Jewish temple and the Catholic Church buildings had this in common: they were both built so that people might spend time with God together. They are specialized buildings. They weren't built for people to watch movies together. That's a different kind of building. And they weren't built so that people could study rats, manufacture legal drugs, build heavy tanks or submarines; those are all a different kind of building. These were buildings designed with the purpose of making a nice house for God to come into and intensify his presence and visit with his human creations in a loving and pleasing way. Just the opposite of the Orange County landscape on a smoggy day.

And each of these buildings, in fact every church and synagogue, has a special small place where God especially packs himself into and hides, and this place is called the sanctuary, and Christians and Jews alike will come into the church or temple to visit more closely with God, and they will go down and get near the sanctuary and sometimes even kneel down in front of where God has compressed and intensified his presence and they will pray there, talk to God, listen to what he answers, or sometimes just sit silently with him and feel his presence.

But if you open the doors to the sanctuary, usually pretty small doors, you will see one thing in a Jewish temple and another thing in a Catholic church. In the Jewish temple sanctuary, God lives in the Torah, which is a parchment scroll of words written in ink, the first five books of the Bible, Genesis, Exodus, Leviticus, Numbers and Laws. In the Catholic Church sanctuary you will find some bread, but unleavened bread, the sort Jesus blessed the night before he died. But God lives in this bread; and to Catholics he is this bread.

So right away we see some differences. You have to be pretty darn smart to learn to read the Torah because it is written in ancient Hebrew, not an easy language to learn. And the words are piled high and overflowing with meaning, all the stories of Adam and Eve and Cain and Abel and Noah and Abraham and Joseph and Moses, and the ten commandments, and all the laws, and the prophecies that the Jews are the Chosen People; all that and much more is there in the sanctuary with God radiating out of it. And you have to be smart, and usually thirteen years old to understand enough of what is in the sanctuary, and to interpret some of the Bible in your Bar Mitzvah Day Speech, and to even read and hold the Torah.

And in the Catholic church sanctuary there is unleavened bread in small pieces sitting on some sort of plate, and that bread is believed to be God, and some say the whole creation and more is contained in each of those little pieces of bread, not that far from William Blake's idea about a grain of sand, only more palatable. And you don't have to be that smart to believe you are eating God when you are eating the bread; in fact it helps to be a little childlike at the moment you do it, even if you are in your nineties. And the Catholic Church feels you are ready to eat the bread when you are seven, and very much a child; that you have enough understanding by then to get intimate with God in that way.

So here are two different paths leading toward God. And the Jews are on one path and the Catholics are on another. One sees the Torah as the way, and the other remembers Jesus when he said, "I am the way."

And Jews, who are trained to be smart from the get-go, gave us Jesus, Mary, Joseph, Peter, Paul and so on, and when that Golden Age was over they gave us Einstein, Marx, Freud, and perhaps a bit of Darwin, so post-Biblical Jews have definitely been chosen, among many other wonderful things, to be great thinkers that influence our world.

And Catholics gave us Jesus, Mary, Joseph, Peter, Paul and so on, and when that Golden Age was over they gave us Joan of Arc, Mother Teresa, and, in a loose sense, Martin Luther King. These post-Biblical folks were known less for their thinking and more for their goodness in action.

And God, if there is a God, made all of us.

4

Money

Inside the mind of each of us runs a long thin boundary with money on one side and God on the other. Funny that so many people question God's existence; yet no one questions the existence of money. We assume it is bedrock real, without a doubt. We doubt witches are real, or goblins, and we laugh at primitive people who run scared from spirits in the woods. We say: No, God, witches, demons, goblins, ghosts, they only exist in peoples' heads. But money is real, without dispute.

And we build countless large brick banks, with impermeable steel vaults deep within, and only the priestly class of bankers knows the combinations to these chambers, these sanctuaries that contain neither Torah nor consecrated bread, only money in its myriad forms. And the banks are built so that people may better commune with this strange and, in some very real sense, very unreal thing called money.

Let us imagine for a moment that all humanity suddenly perished from the earth.

The bears would remain and the bulls, the lions and the fish, the soaring birds, the trees and the boulders, and the sea and the sun. And they would continue to shit in the woods, mount the cows, eat the lambs, grow pine cones that turned into new trees, roll down the mountains, and fly above the fish-filled waters in both daylight and dark of night.

But what of money, if man suddenly became extinct? Money could only lie inert and meaningless, entombed in the bank vaults and the wallets of corpses, until it moldered; only the metal coins would long survive, and they would seldom be moved.

No matter what else you think of money, you must admit it is dead without man's imagination and belief. Its only life is the life it lives in the minds of people and their shared agreements and credos.

But if God exists he can damn well exist without our cooperation, thank you, and keep an awe-inspiring universe sailing along without our joining in, if he chooses. There is fire and rain with or without man, and earth and air will still go on if man leaves the stage, but money disappears and ceases to seem alive if and when we poor souls do.

In this sense money lacks the potential for the sort of reality God has, if God does indeed exist.

Many people admit to believing, though some somewhat grudgingly, that a man named Jesus was actually born two thousand years ago, and that he lived, broke bread, pissed in the desert wind, grew calluses on his hands carpentering and calluses on his feet walking from town to town in the dry and sometimes mountainous Israel of his day. They would also probably concede that he shot off his mouth a lot, and that though his deeds and ideas eventually so enraged the political and religious power group of the time that they had him executed, he nevertheless spoke words that were often profound and truthful, and therefore worth something still, even if they believe the rest of his life story has been exaggerated beyond belief by his overly zealous and blinded followers.

It is therefore worth noting that the Gospels report Jesus said a man must either serve God or money. And that not one of us can serve both.

This axiom appears in the short declaration by Jesus that no one can be a slave of two masters: that he will either hate the first and love the second, or be attached to the first and despise the second. He then goes on to say that you, my friend, cannot be the slave of both God and of money.

And isn't this somewhat of a surprise and worth thinking about a while? That he did not say a human being's choice was between good and evil. Or between virtue and vice. Or even between God and the Devil. These would be the words we might have expected from him.

No, the choice was between serving one master or another, and the two masters he mentioned are God and money.

And if this choice is real for all of us as the words proclaim, if these words of Jesus are words at the least of a very wise man who is speaking some oft-hidden but underlying universal truth, then please ask yourself which master have you chosen, and which master do you presently serve?

Take your time on that question. Go back to it with some frequency. And then answer it as honestly as you can.

FIFTEEN OR TWENTY YEARS ago I visited with two men I had known a while, had lunch with one, and later that day had a long talk with the other. These two men were both in their early fifties, pleasant-looking and intelligent. One was a multi-millionaire and the other was a panhandler.

Roger is the name of the millionaire I have now known for close to fifty years. He is gray and clean-shaven, but when I met him he was young and red-bearded like some glamorous pirate in a movie. At first he intermittently drove a milk truck for a local dairy distributor, and sometimes he just bummed around with his buddies, all of whom were fresh out of college and trying to live the happy dreams of 1960s' pop culture, dreams of love, sex, drugs, and nature, dreams that were far from what was then the rat race and constraints of our mainstream capitalistic culture.

After his period as would-be flower child had passed, he went abroad to Kuwait and taught English to the rich for five years, and then on to Hawaii for three years as a university employee instructing prospective ESL (English as a second language) teachers.

Another friend and I pried Roger loose from his Hawaiian idyll with promises of making millions in our amino acid business, but that venture failed, and so, after floundering a while, he began setting up his own amino acid enterprise, began it as a mail order company operating out of his rather seedy studio apartment.

When sales grew, he moved to a modest townhouse and kept his little but growing moneymaker contained in the larger of two upstairs bedrooms. He added an employee, and then another employee. And when his enterprise continued to flourish he moved it out of his home and into an industrial building, and then in a few years to an even larger industrial building, and hired more and more employees, and he left his home in the rented townhouse and bought a rather palatial house and grounds in a locked and gated community in the country with a community pool, hot tub, tennis courts, sauna. He married, and after five years she left him, and she was given a settlement that retired her for life, and Roger now lived alone except for two or three loving and friendly dogs, and he lived very much beneath his means, and his business continued to slowly grow, and Roger had accomplished much of what is called the American dream, although by now of course it is more the International dream.

During our lunch together Roger spoke of his initially exciting venture into the stock market that had taken place the previous year. For some time, Roger had been putting portions of his hard-earned money into stocks and bonds with the thought of eventual retirement, but for the past year he had found himself wanting to learn much more about investing with the hope of becoming richer, financially, than he had ever been or even dreamed of being.

And so he studied with people who knew the stock market, and he read books and articles on the market, and set aside a hundred thousand dollars of his savings as a grub stake. Then he sat down at his computer each morning, because his business was now staffed with people who could largely run it without him, and he stayed at his computer playing the market until the afternoon, and he did this for over a year, learning, making mistakes, his fortunes rising and falling, but overall rising, until he was sure he could become even far richer than the multi-millions his business had given him. And this was very exciting for him, and it took his mind off the pain caused by his wife's departure, and he found it took his mind off most everything else, and he found that he liked to look at the pages of small numbers the newspapers printed, small numbers telling how all the stocks and bonds were doing and whether they were rising or falling, almost as if they were breathing and growing like living things, or falling ill and sometimes dying like living things, and although they were not really living things he was fascinated by them; and gradually he was fascinated with little else.

As he talked to me Roger brought out his pen and began drawing on the restaurant's paper place mat in front of him. He drew lines and curves and charts to illustrate how stocks and bonds behaved and almost seemed to have lives of their own. He used words like parabola, and indexes, and futures, and many other words I didn't understand, and the lines and curves on the napkin didn't represent anything that I could recognize, nothing like a house or a tree; in fact they looked relatively meaningless, but he drew them and spoke of them heatedly, though with no trace of joy.

Then he went on to tell me that during this current year, which was then about three-quarters over, he had continued last year's life-consuming obsession with stocks and bonds and money and that to his surprise he had lost every cent of his stock market winnings a few months ago, the culmination of a long slide in bad or unlucky decisions, and that all the time and learning and effort and hopes and excitement he'd whirled around in for close to two years had ended with nothing to show for themselves but the experience itself and his gratitude for being able to stop without running the real risk of going under and losing something or all of the larger fortune he'd been lucky enough to amass in business.

He told me the whole thing had been a long descent into addiction, and that now with the addiction lifted he was left in a psychological state that held no real sense of vitality, or even purpose. His business was calling out its demands for his creativity and motivation but he no longer felt creative or motivated (the addict's post-high crash).

I told him I thought it might be time to see a good psychotherapist, and he told me he was already seeing one.

He told me he felt God had spared him from a success that in retrospect seemed empty and without any real substance. I asked him if he felt he had been serving God or money during that time, and without hesitation he told me he had been serving money.

THIS IS A STORY of humanity and the stock market that *Time* magazine doesn't tell. *Time* has no "Bad Trip of the Week" feature for money, like they had for LSD in the 1960s.

There are worse money trips, I know. How about the one that was taken decades ago in Georgia when a professional trader took a rapid plummet into deep stock market debt and killed his wife and children and a number of fellow stock market employees, and of course the whole thing was attributed to anything other than an addiction to money, which is the most pervasive and toxic drug in the universe, that negatively affects more people than any other drug, and ruins more lives, both the lives of the addicts, who unlike Roger are never delivered from their addiction, and the countless poor souls who suffer at their hands.

We will return to money as addictive drug in a while, but let's not forget the panhandler I met at five in the afternoon on the same day I had lunch with Roger.

I don't know the panhandler's name. How many panhandlers have you met and then learned their names? But I knew him quite well by sight and sound because I had seen him often on the streets and park benches of the city, because I worked in the city and walked about a great deal: from my office to the bank, and to the post office, to the coffee shops and stationary stores, the book stores, the markets and drug stores, the theaters and restaurants, walked about the city on my business and recreational errands, tackling life or enjoying it, always with money in my wallet and pockets, and because our city had so many street musicians, street entertainers, and panhandlers standing, sitting, kneeling on the sidewalks I usually carried a dollar or more in quarters because for reasons I don't always understand I want to give away some of this thing called money. And there were some street musicians and panhandlers I never gave to and some I always gave to, and this particular panhandler whose name I don't know but whom I would recognize anywhere was one of those I would almost always give some to.

He was clean, as are most of the non-alcoholic poor on the city's streets, and wore what appeared to be old or secondhand clothes that were neither dirty nor musty.

His costume never varied: black shirt and pants (and a black jacket on colder days), black socks and shoes, and a black baseball cap turned backwards on his head; then black-framed dark glasses, and a black roughly groomed Vandyke beard beginning to gray a little on its edges; and long black hair worn Indian-style with a braid that reached almost to his belt line.

He was a white man and pallid: the color of his skin contrasted sharply with the color of his clothing. So did the two teeth set almost an inch apart at the front of his lower jaw. They were the only teeth visible, rather twisted, serving as small but mildly conspicuous reddish-brown accents to a personal color scheme that was otherwise entirely black and white.

In the months preceding our accidental five o'clock meeting we had spoken briefly on several occasions and I learned he was living off some sort of government dole. He panhandled only when the expense of paying police tickets citing him for living out of his car drove his monthly budget up past the bursting point. But unfortunately this circumstance occurred with some regularity. After he had raised the money to pay these unexpected debts to our proper society, I would see him in the park sitting on a bench by the duck pond apparently enjoying his hours of leisure, silence, and solitude.

Our extended meeting happened in this way: When lunch with the wealthy but rather despondent and dazed Roger had ended, I returned to work and saw clients the rest of the day. Then I went to the library and ordered a two-week stack of a neighboring city's newspaper because a friend of mine who knew I was writing on the subject of money had phoned to tell me a star high school football player, in expectation of being great some day, had tattooed a large dollar sign on his chest. An article and accompanying picture had appeared in the last couple of weeks, but my friend wasn't sure on what day.

As I waited for a library page to bring the papers, my panhandler acquaintance appeared and then came my way, sat down, and began to talk. He told me things had gone bad for him of late, gone bad inside himself, and that he found he had by now erected a psychological wall that kept him from other people. He wasn't sure why, perhaps because he had been hurt so much by others. He had never felt this way before and he wasn't sure what to make of his condition, this completely cut-off feeling, and a certain lifelessness.

The more he talked the better he seemed to feel. To my surprise he took off his dark glasses for the first time in our relationship and revealed a pair of warm and soulful suffering blue eyes, and for the first time we enjoyed eye contact together. Then, another first: he took off his hat and revealed the top of his head, with abundant hair, just beginning to gray, that fed into the long braid.

By now he was talking freely and enjoying himself. He told me a lawyer had found him mentally incompetent and the courts had appointed a guardian to manage his funds, but the guardian turned out to be a professional prostitute and only used her other, more respectable, career as a cover for the real source of her earnings. It was this woman's friends and acquaintances who had so harassed and assaulted his emotions that he entered the strange psychological shell he originally complained of to me.

Next he launched into a long story of how he had once gone thirty-five days without any money at all, not even a penny. It began in California the day he found himself wishing to visit some relatives in Michigan. He set out with empty pockets in the summertime, taking nothing with him other than the clothes he had on: jeans and a T-shirt, socks, underwear, and a pair of tennis shoes.

He told me with some pride that he had never once asked anyone for a meal or money during this trip and yet somehow food had come his way, or did so until once, near the end of his journey, when he had spent just over five days without eating, nary a crumb. That night, on the outskirts of a small town, he broke into an elementary school cafeteria and to his delight found and then stole a large jar of peanut butter and two loaves of bread. He took his plunder to a nearby graveyard and feasted at his leisure before bedding down among the tombstones.

And so within a single day I was exposed to two personal accounts that focused on money matters. Neither man was on the extreme edge of the economic curve: Roger was no multi-billionaire, and the man in black was not starving to death on an urban sidewalk or in the dried-out countryside. In some way they belonged to the same group: Those of us who sleep outside of jails and prisons yet manage to eat most every day and aren't forced to beg for every meal. Those of us who have some form of medical care. Those of us who needn't wonder if our children will die in famine before we do.

And neither man was chronically addicted to money.

MONEY ADDICTION ISN'T TALKED about much, but it's a lot like addiction to cocaine, heroin, alcohol, or work except its effects are much much worse, because in the advanced stages of this addiction you will do anything to get more of what you so fiercely crave. Hard-core money addicts can remain addicted for a lifetime, and may die still consumed and sickened by their spiritual disease.

A hard-core money addict will lie, rob, cheat, steal, physically hurt people, kill people, and will do this day after day and year after year. And if you have lots of money and are addicted to it, really lots and lots of money, you can do all these evil things on an insanely large scale, and do them legally; and you will, and you do.

That is, unless you are rich from being at the top of a drug cartel. Because then you and your underlings can do all of these terrible things to people, but you can't do them legally, so the newspapers will be against you, and you will go to jail as soon as the few police and judges you haven't bribed with money or fear get hold of you.

But if your dealings with international death are done in a legal way, say with manufactured cigarettes or major killings on the stock or packaged loan market, or the right kind of war, you can make immense killings and only be curtailed a little bit in your home base, which leaves all of Asia and all the underdeveloped countries to lie to (advertise, editorialize) and murder in without much impediment, and really only slow and relatively minor obstacles are encountered at home because the government at home is also largely addicted to money and serving money more than God or people. And why would you leave Harvard Business School and hire on with a cigarette company or a major military equipment manufacturer if you weren't simply interested in money? Or for that matter, hire on with an oil company, a stock trader or gun manufacturer? To make the world a better place?

Unlike their approach to alcohol and drug addiction, the newspapers and television don't talk much, if at all, about hard-core murderous money addiction, and don't really seem at all incensed if and when they do.

So the public isn't stirred up about you that much, or angry, or wanting to revolt against you, throw you out of office, change the laws that govern you (which are the laws you yourselves usually get to write just now).

In fact the public is hypnotized into a state of looking up to you. You, the money addict, the most dangerous addict of all, the one who may really be serving money almost all the time, and not serving God much at all if ever, one of the ones that Dante placed nearer to the bottom of Hell than those who were merely addicted to something like lusting after the flesh, perhaps because flesh is real, and God-given, and doesn't just exist in the minds of men like money does.

A decade or more ago, in a Sunday newspaper supplement, an article appeared with a full-color painting of a small man watering a large green tree, and the tree is not growing leaves, it's growing money; and the green paper money leaves, in various denominations, are photographed rather than painted so as to look more real than the rest of the picture, and they are packed on in abundance to give the money tree a full-foliage luxuriant look.

The article is boldly titled "Making the Most of Your 401(k)."

Have you seen any 401(k)s lately? Helped any 401(k)s across the street? The language of money is so strange, and so inhuman. It is not about anything real and simple like eating peanut butter sandwiches at night after a long period of fasting. Money, unlike food, exists only in our communal minds, and some of us believe in it more than we believe in apples.

A long ago front page headline read, "Dow-ner Average falls 524.30 for the week, setting record decline." Something dramatic has been reported, but the language is so specialized and un-childlike that it's difficult to visualize what is going on here. A falling stone, a falling star, yes, I can see that. A falling average? A record falling average? A Dow-ner? This is obviously the secret language of some mad priestly class, the priests who intone over money in bank vaults, speaking the sacred Latin of our day. The holy words of the thing that only exists when man does, fallen man on a Dow-ner.

And then on the business page, another headline, "Dow spirals downward. Troubled investors still selling." Not good news, clearly. Something is spiraling downward. Some people are troubled, the investors are troubled. The troubled investors are selling. But what? Peanut butter? Bathtubs? Something real? Anything real here? 401(k).

AND NOW DEAR READER, GENTLE READER—I know this is mostly a book of memoirs and a book of times gone by, but let's step into the present a moment—the year is now 2014.

It's about six years after that big economic crash, the recent one in which the United States government bailed out a number of corporate crooks at a cost of over a trillion dollars to the taxpayers and treasury.

But nobody went to jail. No millionaires jumped to their deaths from tall buildings. Nobody even gave up their multi-million dollar Christmas bonus.

It is now 2014, and a study by Oxfam concludes that today's eighty-five richest people own the same wealth as the wealth owned by the entire bottom half of our world's population: that's the wealth of over three and a half billion not so rich people.

Oxfam is an international confederation of seventeen organizations working in ninety countries to find solutions to poverty and injustice around the world. Their assessment that the wealth of eighty-five people is equal to the wealth of three billion, five hundred million people, is mind-boggling. For your mind, for my mind, for any human being's mind. For many of us, both mind-boggling and utterly disgusting.

And this recent crash, known as the Great Recession, had a lot in common with the 1920s' crash, the crash that resulted in the Great Depression.

Both crashes occurred during a period of extensive financial law deregulation. The more recent deregulations began under the administration of President Ronald Reagan and his appointee Federal Reserve Chairman Alan Greenspan.

Both crashes involved large-scale crime made legal by unrealistically lax laws, thanks to a federal government owned by Money.

You might want to watch a recent good movie by Robert Reich titled *Inequality For All*. Robert Reich is an economist and author who served in the Ford and Carter administrations and was Secretary of Labor under President Bill Clinton. His movie is about how and why most of us are poorer now, except for a very small group of people who are richer now, among them those few people who own most of the media and most of the government. About half of our congressmen are millionaires now, and just about all of our senators. The government tends to lean towards and serve big corporations, like corporations in the oil industry, drug industry, et cetera, et cetera.

Senator Bernie Sanders of Vermont recently wrote that 95 percent of the new income in this country from 2009–12 went to the top richest 1 percent of our population.

Until very recently, for seven or eight years I lived in Montgomery, Alabama, the state's capital. Not long ago the Montgomery newspaper ran the following headline: "Schwab Launches All-ETF 401(k)." Whatever that means.

AND NOW, BACK TO the older memoirs, from a slightly different age.

A long, long while ago I went looking for Michael. Michael's boss would say Michael was the best worker at the huge price-cutting warehouse store in our town, a gigantic store with food and televisions, computers and clothes, bicycles and almost anything that comes quickly to mind when thinking of what a middle-class person might often want to buy. The store is part of a national chain, a very successful money-making enterprise whose average might have gone down that day causing troubled investors to sell. Michael had worked there a number of years and occupied a position somewhere between his boss and the checkout people. In the army Michael would have been a sergeant.

I went looking for Michael because he had missed his Thursday afternoon appointment. When Michael missed an appointment I was supposed to phone a case manager for the insurance company that pays for Michael's therapy, because Michael was an alcoholic in remission and the large company that he worked for paid the insurance company to make sure that he kept his therapy appointments. If I phoned the case manager she would phone Michael's boss, so I phoned Michael after he missed his Thursday appointment to avoid snitching on him, but he didn't answer the phone, and then I phoned him on Friday, but he didn't answer, so I wrote him a note and then went looking for him at the downtown residential hotel where he rented a room, and where I could at least leave the note with the hotel manager.

This was the first time I'd been inside the hotel, which looks very nice in the lobby and on the mezzanine where the manager's office was located. The manager's office door had a card that informed me I'd arrived too late but that night managers were on duty in residential rooms on the second and fifth floors. So I got into the elevator which was rundown and didn't work right and wouldn't take me to the second floor at all but did take me to the fifth floor. That manager wasn't there, but I did see the hotel was seedy, drab, dark, and rundown.

When I at last got to the second floor, this time more successfully riding the slow elevator with its flaking walls and peeling carpet, I found a night manager, and there inside the small dark room, visiting the night manager was Larry, the gardener for the building that houses my office.

Larry had once been named the best high school football player in the state of Louisiana, and like Michael he was a recovering alcoholic. Larry had two years of sobriety. The night manager advised me to come back Monday and gave my note to the day manager.

Larry said goodbye to the night manager and rode downstairs with me and we visited a while in front of the hotel. Gardening our building is just part-time work for Larry. He recently found a job at a lumberyard. He told me he started at ten dollars an hour, has gone up to twelve dollars and fifty cents an hour, and now has health insurance, as well as credit for a week's vacation. He also told me that he doesn't care about money, only about Christ, and that he is a very happy man. He just wants to live in Christ and die in Christ, and he was going home to his wife now. I believed him.

About fifteen years ago I read that the four richest men in America had a combined wealth that amounted to more than the gross national product of China. But then, how many peanut butter sandwiches can you eat? Now that the rich are taxed less in our country, and their incomes are racing away from those of the people they employ, they can put something away for a rainy day. But I doubt Michael and Larry can.

When I grew up in Los Angeles in the late 1930s and '40s the summer skies were always blue, and I had time to lie down in our small neighborhood park and look up at them. There were lots of mosquitoes in those days, but they shared the clear air with all sorts of butterflies: Tiger Swallowtails, Mourning Cloaks, Monarchs; even the Buckeye Moths were colorful.

To travel outside the neighborhood we often mounted our trusty bicycles and pedaled north all the way to the Hollywoodland sign in the mountains that bordered the city, and there surveyed the view, or rode south all the way to the Baldwin Hills, and there shot our BB guns at the rabbits that lived in the furrowed acres of bean bushes that were farmed in the area.

Nobody got killed or injured and it was safe to ride because the traffic was light enough, although one boy, Bobby, I forget his last name, got killed by a streetcar that ran along our boulevard, a boulevard with not that many cars and even a few horse-drawn rag pickers' wagons, and a horse-drawn ice truck.

The streetcar that killed Bobby was part of a large system of streetcars that ran the east-west lengths of the city and beyond. The so-called Red Car Line in front of our house ran from the ocean twenty miles west of us to the San Gabriel Mountains thirty miles east of us. When my family moved from our old home to a larger place some miles north, we were served by the Yellow Car Line, which did roughly the same thing the Red Cars did, only the Yellow Cars were more modern. Both cost a dime a ride.

When you wanted to travel north-south in the city you transferred to a bus, so you could go virtually anywhere in Los Angeles or its suburbs for a dime because the transfers were free, and that meant a movie downtown would take twenty cents round trip for a half-hour ride (it takes about the same amount of time by car now), and the streetcars and buses ran about every three minutes during the daytime.

But then the hard-core money addicts that ran the big oil companies and the big auto companies got together and paid for a very expensive and very destructive lie. They invented a number of so-called "transportation companies" with very real sounding names and those puppet companies bought up the Red Car Line and the Yellow Car Line and all the other streetcar lines that served Los Angeles so well, and once the money addicts owned those lines they just tore up their streetcar tracks and scrapped them, trashed the streetcars, and repaved the roads so you would never know streetcars had run there. And so suddenly, unless you had a car you were shit out of luck, and the cars came like the mosquitoes had once come and overran the city, and the blue skies vanished into tailpipe exhaust fumes, and after a while we had DDT (a petroleum byproduct) and the mosquitoes and butterflies were gone for good, and the clear air was gone with smog replacing it, and I suppose the whole disastrous and sickening change probably came out of money addiction, else why would they do it—ruin a perfectly good city and leave its population coughing with smarting eyes and traffic snarls and used car lots and gray skies that had once been blue.

Oh, yes, and a public radio science commentator just said it was insecticides that were killing off the honeybees, thereby threatening plant life and our agricultural system and market.

In the late 1960s, my brother, who is a doctor, told me that the smog in

Los Angeles made living there equivalent to smoking a pack of cigarettes a day. So the money addicts had little kids and old people smoking a pack of cigarettes a day whether they wanted to or not, and because I had a couple of children by then I left my hometown for a place where we could breathe safely, and one without daily gridlock. I was, along with millions of others, a victim of money addicts, and now a refugee from the kind of damage they will do to feed their most pernicious of addictions.

I met Peter Carota when he was seventeen, and after he finished college Peter became a Realtor, and soon after that a real estate broker. Through a combination of smartness, goodness, charisma, and providential breaks, Peter had made enough money and bought enough property to retire at the age of twenty-six.

He lived in a home with surrounding acreage on our county's fashionable Day Valley Road. He owned a Mercedes-Benz, but for the most part he lived simply, although he would go to Europe whenever he felt like it, took all the classes like music, art, drama and dance that he hadn't had time for in college, and finally got a little bored and went down to Brazil and found himself working in the slums with the very poor. He underwent a powerful religious conversion, and then came back and got very active in the Catholic Church for the first time in his adult life.

And after he returned from Brazil with a newfound power to his faith, Peter was unsure about what he wanted to do in life, and while he was pondering, an old friend of his named Mrs. Green came down with cancer. Mrs. Green was a rich and devout Catholic lady, perhaps seventy years old, and a widow without heirs whose impressive financial fortunes many were courting, including our local Catholic hospital. The sicker Mrs. Green got, the more she relied on Peter, and eventually he moved into her home in Santa Cruz. And Peter called up a lady doctor he had worked with in the slums of Brazil and the doctor came and stayed with Peter and Mrs. Green and they focused on helping Mrs. Green in the last months of her life.

The more virulent Mrs. Green's cancer became, the more she talked about wanting to see the face of God. This became her singular and strong goal. Her illness progressed to where she weighed little more than her own skeleton, and Peter had to carry her from place to place in her home, and the doctor ministered to her medically because Mrs. Green was suffering a tormenting degree of physical distress and pain.

At last Mrs. Green told Peter and the doctor that she would die on the next Thursday, which was then about five days away. When Thursday came she didn't die, but she did slip into a coma from which she never fully emerged. On that Thursday, after being in the coma for several hours, she began speaking excitedly about seeing the face of God, and she was indeed seeing it as she spoke. Her face was radiating ecstatic joy, and she kept crying out, "It's beautiful! It's beautiful! It's so beautiful."

Then Mrs. Green became very silent and peaceful and two days later she died.

Somewhat to Peter's surprise, Mrs. Green left half of her money to him. Now Peter was even richer than before, and in crisis as to what to do with his money. After much deliberation he decided to follow St. Francis into poverty, and he gave away or sold all his belongings, and spent all of his past and new financial holdings opening St. Francis Catholic Kitchen, which is a large place where our city's homeless and poor could be fed one substantial meal every day.

Later Peter opened Jesus, Mary and Joseph Home, an institution that provided food and lodging for the homeless and helped them to find work and become independent. Peter himself remained in voluntary poverty and lived at these facilities in a small room for a number of years, and then he was ready to begin yet another chapter in his life.

Peter entered a Catholic seminary and became a priest. He now works with the poor in a dry rural town a hundred and fifty miles away from where the soup kitchen and homeless housing are still going strong. By the time he entered the seminary he was forty-one years old. By the time he became a priest he was forty-eight.

Peter has demonstrated an ability to focus and succeed in the world, and Peter did not suffer an addiction to money.

THE *New Yorker* MAGAZINE ran an article some years ago that began with President Bill Clinton deliberating over whether to spend a billion dollars to pay for more of a particular type of Patriot missile. He was thinking of using this type of missile in our growing missile-defense system. The missile manufacturer's stock had gone up just at the possibility of such a windfall in business.

The missile already had a wartime track record. In January 1991 General Norman Schwarzkopf Jr., American commander of the first Gulf War, claimed the success rate for the Patriot to be 100 percent: thirty-three of these missiles had thus far been fired, and thirty-three Iraqi Scuds (another type of missile—ours were Patriots, theirs were Scuds) aimed at Israel had been destroyed. So said the General.

By February 1991, forty-two of these missiles had been fired at Scuds, and President George H. W. Bush made a speech claiming that of those forty-two launchings, forty-one resulted in interceptions. That's a 98 percent success rate. Bush allowed that no system is perfect, "But Patriot is proof positive that missile defense works."

At the end of the Gulf War, the Army was claiming a 96 percent success rate for the Patriot.

But then some man-with-a-mission social oddball began diligently investigating the claims of super efficiency for the missiles. At first both the Army and the plant that made the missiles responded with stonewalling, and when that didn't work, they shifted to spreading ugly and untrue rumors about the man's life and character.

Finally, in the face of his growingly successful attempts to uncover the truth behind their lies, the Army backed down with an admission that maybe the missile efficiency was only 80 percent. Then they backed down to 70 percent. Eventually it turned out that the whole gaggle of missiles, all of them, for which we taxpayers had spent at least hundreds of millions of dollars, probably hadn't so much as hit one single solitary target, and that the only damage they inflicted occurred when their exploded gargantuan bodies fell in scattered piles of metal on the cities and countryside, the very places they had been launched to protect.

When this truly independent private citizen contacted President Bush's office (President Bush never deigned to communicate with him personally), the presidential office official informed him that the words "intercept" or "interception" meant only that the trajectory of the missile had crossed the trajectory of its target. No contact between the missile and target whatsoever. Never. On no occasion. This is what 41 out of 42 interceptions meant.

As President Bush noted, no system is perfect.

Do you suppose the builders of these total duds didn't know what had happened? Or the military? Or the president? Or the next president who was pondering whether to buy another billion dollars worth of fantasy? Fantasies that ended up hurting the people and places they were purchased to defend. Not to bring into question the motives behind the dirty Gulf War in the first place. This is money addiction as practiced among the thickest, densest levels of money, where corruption and immorality thrive on their diet of practiced large-scale deceit and lies.

ABOUT A HUNDRED YEARS ago a young Dutchman who was perfectly healthy and good-looking, smart and hard-driving, decided to live on an island where the local government stored its lepers. If you contacted leprosy in those days you were involuntarily shipped off to this island, and you and the other lepers were pretty much on your own, and being left there that way the whole population had drifted into social chaos, kind of a living hell, except the people condemned to it weren't especially sinful, and very few if any of them had been addicted to money or anything else really bad. They were more of a social cross section, but all of them had had the misfortune of contacting leprosy, no different than all the people who randomly contract many physically tragic conditions, like suddenly getting a brain tumor.

The island, which was in Hawaii, was named Molokai. The handsome, healthy, industrious young Dutchman was named Damien. Actually, Father Damien—he was a Catholic priest on his first Church assignment, one he had volunteered for.

When he got to the island the smell there was awful, both from the rotting flesh of the living lepers, and the rotting flesh of the leprous corpses that were piled up above ground and simply left to decompose.

So the first thing Damien did was to get a shovel and start digging deep graves. He dug all day and then slept outdoors, and after two weeks he was tired and sore but all the bodies were interred.

Then he went to work putting the rest of the island's society in order and he saw to it that the lepers had decent places to live for the first time, decent recreation, a decent place to worship, and decent hospitalization and medical care. He had the lepers doing most of the work, and that gave them purpose and a sense of accomplishment, plus a sense of helping themselves. There were even a number of church weddings.

One man, Father Damian, changed a lot of people's lives and made a lot of people happy.

If he lied to them at all it was by telling them that there was a God who loved them, and that this God had a son named Jesus who loved them, too, and who had lived and died for them. But then this may not have been a lie. It may have been true, and certainly Father Damien believed it was true, and look at all the good that came from it.

Father Damien stayed on Molokai for decades and after a while he discovered he, too, had leprosy. Little by little his disease advanced until he could no longer walk or even move much and he was covered with open sores and his flesh and body were rotting off of him, and finally he died on the island he had saved, himself a victim of the illness he had come to minister to.

Father Damien never once suffered from the worse disease, the addiction to money. He died truly happy, joyful, and exuberantly healthy in the part of himself where health counts most.

My wife's cousin Lois died about twelve years ago. Lois had been a lovely woman who spent her youth in the same small town in which my wife was growing up. Their mothers were sisters, and Lois and my wife grew up more like sisters than cousins, spending lots of time together, laughing and talking, sleeping over, and being close girlhood friends.

Then Lois got married and went off to live with her husband who was a career military man, and the two of them had a child together, and when Lois turned fifty they were about ready to retire to a lakeside where they had bought property. But then Lois got a brain tumor.

The doctors operated on Lois and removed the tumor, but another tumor grew, and so they took that one out; and then another tumor grew, and Lois was getting tired and beat-up from the effects of the surgeries and medicines and the tumors themselves, and three years after the first tumor came, Lois lay down and died.

One thing about Lois, aside from being a good wife, mother, worker, and friend, was that she loved diet sodas and drank them all the time, and had been doing so ever since they came on the market.

Diet sodas are often sweetened with aspartame, which is the name for aspartic acid and phenylalanine when they are bonded together, and the technical name for both NutraSweet and Equal. Because diet sodas are so popular, megatons of aspartame, a relatively new invention, go into the making of them. Phenylalanine is an amino acid, and when I was selling amino acids I was told by a doctor that taking large amounts of phenylalanine was associated with getting brain tumors.

60 Minutes, the television show, ran a report on aspartame just a little under twenty years ago. They pointed out that there has been a steady rise in the number of people who are coming down with fatal brain tumors, and that the rise began just about the same time aspartame entered the marketplace.

They also pointed out that the number of people getting brain tumors is going up at about the same rate as the tonnage of aspartame being sold (used in diet sodas, some ice teas, yogurts, pancake syrups, soft drinks, and so on). If you drew a graph, the lines for both aspartame sales and brain tumor occurrence would be going up steeply, and basically on the same trajectory.

Of course, the makers of aspartame are getting tons of money for selling it, and more every summer that goes by, even while the doctors are getting money performing all those surgeries, and we weren't hearing much that is scary about aspartame in the diet soda ads, or in press releases from the medical establishment, either.

60 Minutes reported that so far as they knew there had been a hundred and sixty-four research projects to see if aspartame use is related to the onset of cancerous brain tumors, and that seventy-four of those studies were funded by the NutraSweet (aspartame) industry, and that every one of those industry-funded studies said aspartame was safe. But of the other ninety studies, that were funded independently, eighty-three identified a problem. You can draw your own conclusion.

Part of what troubles me is how the executives and MBAs at the aspartame business can go on drawing money for their work and withholding the facts from the diet-soda-drinking public. Maybe they took lessons from the tobacco company people. Also, how does our government, which leaped out and imprisoned the totally innocent tryptophan, live with itself? And finally, why doesn't the media make more of a story out of this? I never heard a word about it again after the *60 Minutes* presentation.

I suspect it's because the media is in the business of getting most of their money from big companies' advertisements, and they don't want to risk offending Diet Coke and Diet Pepsi, for example, especially because those companies are owned by larger companies that own other big advertisers, like Taco Bell, Doritos, Kentucky Fried Chicken, and so on.

The major media presents itself as being in the business of providing news and truth, but actually it is in the business of becoming super rich by sucking up gobs of advertising money from huge corporations, and that seems to almost invariably involve withholding truth, or lying.

And the government, which has rapidly become the government of the money, for the money, and by the money, is not going to trample on the feelings or frustrate the strategies of its major contributors, which usually include huge corporations, and if the truth isn't out, and right isn't done, we aren't going to lose that many votes from the uninformed possible brain tumor victims of aspartame and their relatives.

So at the top of our economic social order we have a lot of money addicts and money addiction, but as is the case with most dangerous and destructive addictions, the addicts are doing their best to keep their dirty secret a secret and hypnotize us into thinking that what is good for them is what's good for America.

And then there's Rusty and Charlie.

Rusty is a tall redheaded man who looked more like a grown-up Opie from the *Andy Griffith Show* than Ron Howard does. Rusty was married with young children and for fun he liked to compete with racecars that he built and then raced. He even built smaller cars for his children to take onto the track when things were quiet out there.

To get money Rusty owned and ran "Rusty's Honda-Mazda" in Santa Cruz, California. It was a five-bay auto shop and all the mechanics wore blue T-shirts with "Rusty's Honda-Mazda" written over their chest pockets in small white lettering, and they always looked relaxed yet at the same time focused on what they were doing.

When we bought a used Mazda some years ago someone told me about Rusty's and I always went there afterwards.

Rusty was a pleasant man, a very fine mechanic, and honest. He saw to it that we got very good mechanical service at a reasonable price. My Mazda was still running strong when it was twenty years old. Mechanically it could have gone another ten years easily, and its only vulnerability was what would happen if someone did something like rear-ending me, or worse yet, a heavy blow to the side, because the insurance companies would have Blue Booked me out at around $1,700 and the parts alone would have probably cost more than that.

Lots of times when I brought my Mazda in with something real minor Rusty went out and fixed it for free.

We had a Toyota, too, and it was about ten years old, but Rusty wouldn't help us with that car. He was a true specialist, and he knew the limits of his rare excellence and expertise. I liked that.

Rusty got income from a business washed-over and flooded with good will. You could feel it when you went there, or even felt good just thinking about the place in the days in between your routine oil changes.

But I started by saying, "And then there's Rusty and Charlie."

Charlie used to build and remodel houses. At age seventy-nine he still kept his hand in the trade by doing jobs that didn't involve building permits. Charlie got out of those other sorts of larger jobs because he couldn't tolerate the growing bureaucratic hurdles associated with larger construction projects.

I met Charlie more than thirty-five years ago when the bank that was lending us money to build a house said they knew of this contractor that no one had complained about in fourteen years and that that was a rare and unique circumstance. So Charlie and his partner Everett and his helper

Tim and his roofer Dusty built our house for us, and I kept on knowing him afterwards.

Charlie was raised on a farm in Minnesota and then came out to San Francisco as a young man and met Alice, the woman he married, the mother of his four grown children, and the love of his growingly long life. Charlie was a cook in a downtown cafeteria then, but the couple later moved to our small city when Charlie's uncle offered him a job on a housing development that was starting here.

Charlie learned to do all the carpentry on these houses with just hand tools. I guess that's how it was done in those days.

When we talked sometimes it seemed like Charlie built about every tenth house in this town, and that he remembered his relationship with every one of the home owners.

Once I drove through a rich neighborhood and saw a big house that was being remodeled and it had Charlie's contractor's sign out in front, and I found Charlie inside working away on a rather lavish stone kitchen counter. He told me the remodel was a three-quarter million dollar project. That was a lot of money in those days thirty-plus years ago, and I know Charlie made a lot of money. He wasn't working for money those days at all, but just for the love of doing what he did best and so well.

My wife brought back an old rusty broken saw that her grandfather once used many years ago on his own farm, and as a present to her Charlie got all the rust off the saw blade, then polished it and had it sharpened. He patched the broken handle so well you would never know there was once a piece as big as your thumb missing from it, and then he sanded and refinished the handle, too.

The saw looks like a deeply burnished antique work of art now, so we keep it on our piano bench like a Stradivarius violin.

Have you ever dreamed of flying down to Rio? Sugarloaf and Bahia, with swirling mosaic sidewalks and bronzed rolling flesh in topless bikinis, rumba, white sands and warm ocean, all sorts of fine restaurants and food, and fine shops and fine people.

But what if there were too many pigeons in that glorious city, or worse yet, too many rats, and they were making big nuisances of themselves, especially in the moneyed zones where the rich hang out and the tourists spend their savings most heavily?

Then we'd expect the responsible folks who look after such things to take care of the problem quietly, and we hope efficiently.

And if small flocks of pigeons were poisoned to thin out the overcrowded populations, or large bunches of rats trapped and drowned? Surely the health of the city is more important than those small and insignificant lives.

Yet, what if the pests weren't pigeons or rats but, rather, children? Boys and girls from seven to seventeen. What if children were getting in the way of the rich folks having a good time? Would you still want them murdered?

Brazil is the fifth-largest industrialized country in the world, and of its almost two hundred million citizens half are under the age of eighteen. Of those children, at least two or three million live on the streets, usually because a married couple in Brazil who does menial but full-time work earns only enough money to support two people, so their children leave home and fend for themselves by self-employed begging, stealing, and prostitution, or working for adult criminals. Sometimes the waifs go so far as to kill someone to get their money.

These little virtual bastards and their methods of staying fed have a way of making things tough on police, local businessmen, and the local economy, so informal alliances between police, businessmen, and politicians result in death squads which go out and administer vigilante justice, and about fifteen years ago three, four, or five children who live on the streets in Brazil were murdered every day, which adds up to more than a thousand kids a year, more than five thousand in five years, and this is the way things go in Brazil. Not just shooting the kids to death or drowning them like rats, but torturing them to death, beating them to death, often leaving mutilated bodies on some vacant lot or street shoulder.

And this was business as usual, the death squads making up an informal but stable part of the country's economic system, until one night twenty years ago when one death squad opened fire on forty youngsters sleeping on the steps of the Candelaria, Rio de Janeiro's popular cathedral, the place the elite went to worship, a favorite place for weddings, and by tradition a sanctuary for the poor.

Seven or eight children were murdered in that shooting and for a while this was news, and the world cocked a sleepy eye at the goings-on in Brazil. But it was soon forgotten, although sometime later a rare thing happened: Some of the assassins were actually sentenced to jail, and under Brazilian law were sentenced to imprisonment for up to thirty-two years, which comes out to about four years a child. But then this was an exception and the killings go on, I guess for the economy's sake, an economy where most everyone is so poor that millions of kids are better off taking their chances on the murderous streets than starving to death at their working parents' home.

You can go online and get a somewhat more current version of this situation. The figures still aren't quite up to date, and there are explanations about why an accurate number is so hard to find. But the last census for street children in Brazil seems to have been in 2006, when the estimated number of children living on Brazil's streets was twelve million. At that time, the usual fee for having a Brazilian street child killed was fifty dollars.

I HAVE SEEN THE Devil twice in my life.

The first time was in Mexico City when I was twenty-six years old. I saw the Devil a night or two after I was discharged from a hospital where I'd spent some days under an oxygen tent because of a near-fatal case of pneumonia, the sickness having been brought on by a week-long methedrine binge, a binge in which I neither ate nor slept for four or five days, then found myself almost unable to get off my bed and make a phone call asking for help from some kindly relatives who lived less than ten miles away. These people took me straight to a hospital.

After the hospital discharged me back into the care of my relatives, I went to convalesce a while in a large studio apartment that was built into the garage level of their handsome home in one of the wealthiest sections of town. They were very loving people, very generous, and I still remember the kindness they showed me during that very needy hour.

It was on the first or second night in their home that I saw the Devil. The room I occupied was wondrously large, but somehow the Devil was larger, and though he was seated on a ledge above me, with one of his legs fully extended, and the other tucked up to his chest, his physical massiveness and, by comparison, my puniness, were all too apparent for my comfort. I should guess his height to have been fourteen feet, were he standing.

His instant arrival was a complete surprise to me as I had never seen him before, nor had anything in my life led me to expect that I ever would, or prepared me for such an occasion. Yet there he was, towering above me, looking for all the world like some giant colonial aristocrat, with a bouffant white linen shirt, tan breeches and white hosen, one giant foot showing, shod with a shiny black silver-buckled shoe, the other foot hidden behind his massive extended leg. His long reddish hair was styled in the fashion of an off-duty American Constitution signer, and his face was clean-shaven.

I knew this was the Devil with the same certainty I had known God when God first made himself known to me. In the moment there is nothing but knowing who has appeared. The doubts come afterwards, to be pondered and dealt with over the months and years as honestly as possible.

I tried to communicate with the Devil, but he instantly outwitted me. I tried again, but he outwitted me before my thought was complete, even as a great chess master might anticipate the move of a novice while the weaker player still held the chess piece in his grip above the chessboard.

I tried a third time to question him but he anticipated and dismissed me before my effort began to form.

Then he disappeared.

I have thought about this meeting often since, and realize that the Devil is never going to be outwitted by any of us on a purely intellectual playing field. I also worry for those who put their entire faith in reason, logic having a hidden dependence on axioms, a dependence that the highly logical often deny. Therefore, logical or not, it is important to know what you believe in and to pick your articles of faith as cautiously and as wisely as you can.

The constitutional signers were reasonable men, and they reasoned themselves right into establishing slavery as a fundamental national law; let's finally face it, folks, they did that only for economic reasons, and those are reasons very dear to the devil's impoverished heart.

TOM GRANT, WHO DIED in his early sixties about ten years ago, first showed his talent for leadership when he started at point guard for his high school's basketball team and they won the state championship. Then Tom went into a seminary to become a priest, but ended up graduating from a secular university in business administration and worked as a shining young executive for Capitol Company, which was owned by Bank of America which was owned by TransAmerica Corporation.

Ronald Reagan had just been elected governor of California and was calling for business leaders to come help him be the best governor he could be—just business leaders, not leaders like Martin Luther King, Bob Dylan, Leonard Bernstein, Mother Teresa; not educational leaders or experts in crime prevention, or anything like that; just guys who knew how to make *da money.*

And TransAmerica sent Tom Grant as their representative and for six months he did have regular meetings with Ronald Reagan, and when Tom left and went back to TransAmerica Ronald Reagan gave him a blue sticker for his license plate and the sticker said, "Thanks," and was signed "Ronald Reagan." Reagan was described by his admiring biographer as charismatic, a great leader, and vacant. Words that might serve in a rough preliminary sketch for the prototypic antichrist.

After some more years at TransAmerica, Tom went to work for Lewis Douglas Company, which was owned by Aetna. Then to a development company in Fresno; then into commercial real estate in Santa Cruz, where, about twenty years after his business career first began, he underwent a religious conversion, one of those sudden conversions that can sometimes come as a startlingly and divine new experience.

Tom was on a weekend retreat for Christian businessmen that began late on a Friday afternoon. Then Saturday morning around eleven o'clock three or four of the guys were praying over him, and Tom, recalling that moment, said, "I suddenly knew without a doubt that God just loved me, and I was forgiven all the sins I had ever committed . . . I bathed in unconditional love that morning, and I wept like a baby, tears of thanksgiving and joy . . . all good."

That was in 1986.

In May 1993 Tom and his wife Rena entered the Franciscan Order of the Roman Catholic Church. They got accepted as members of what's called the Lay Covenant Community. They had to enter into voluntary poverty, so they left their fancy home in the rich neighborhood and sold their belongings and gave the proceeds to the poor.

Then they moved into two small rooms in a Franciscan retreat house.

Seven years later, Tom and Rena were still living a life of poverty with the Franciscans, but Tom, being a leader, had been chosen, along with his wife, to direct a whole seven-state Western region of the lay covenant program, and that involved overseeing a lot of other people living in voluntary poverty at a lot of other retreat houses, parishes, and missions, people who are dedicated to serving others rather than shaking them down for dollars. I think he got room and board and about $3,500 a year.

Tom said of his life then, "I feel like the process is me earning the knowledge of the fullness of God's love." In other words, different than centering on earning money.

THE SECOND TIME I saw the Devil came about fifteen years after his first visit. I was living in my new home in the countryside on the outskirts of town. My wife and sons were gone for the day and I was alone in the home. At one point I got up from the living room couch and went into the bathroom and took a long look in the mirror that ran above our sink counter. I saw myself clearly enough in the mirror, but the me that I saw was a noble lion, the sort of loving lion that would gladly lie down with a lamb, somewhat like the lion in *The Wizard of Oz*, because man-like; but rather than being comic I was heroic and kind, the sort of figure the Greeks might make a God of, or more accurately, the sort of lion the Christians envision when they portray the disciple and Gospel writer, Mark, as king of the beasts.

I looked at my reflection with surprise, awe, and pleasure a while, and then the image in the mirror began breaking down like a mudslide, and transformed itself into something or someone grotesquely ugly and evil, like a moving picture of the portrait Dorian Gray had hidden in his attic, a fleshy putrescent gargoyle, a fiend. I knew I was looking at the Devil. And for a while, I was the Devil or was at least wholly taken over by him. This was far from pleasant. This was horrible and damnable. I staggered back to the couch and sat a long while until I gradually felt myself again. Then I went back and looked into the mirror for a moment or two, and saw only the humdrum me I'd been watching gradually change in barbershop mirrors for forty years, the me I loved and hated, the normal me in whom good and evil, God and the Devil, wage part of their wars on a regular but usually less visible basis.

Jesus says, seek you first the Kingdom of Heaven and all else will be given to you.

Given. Not earned. Not something to hoard. Not something to hide in a bank vault or under a bushel basket. Not something to lie about, scheme about, tear up streetcar tracks or poison cities for.

Seek you first the Kingdom of Heaven. That's all there is to it. No troubled investors, selling.

Seek you first the Kingdom of Heaven. And all else will be given to you. Given. Not stolen. Given. As in gift. Seek you first the Kingdom of Heaven. These are the words of Jesus. And it is within the Kingdom of Heaven where true wealth lives.

I agree with Uncle Nicholas in Boris Pasternak's *Doctor Zhivago*. He says Jesus came to do away with nations: That when he showed up the Jews were the chosen people, and the Philistines and Romans weren't, and that if you were born into one of those other countries you were just shit out of luck because you weren't chosen and you weren't going to be chosen, but after Jesus arrived anyone could be chosen—Irish, Swahili, Russian, anyone—and so in that sense the whole meaning and import of nations or favored nations was dead upon his arrival.

And something similar is said in the novel and motion picture, *The English Patient*, when the heroine tells the dying hero that each individual is a nation, and that individual human beings are the only real nations in the world. And the hero is dying from injuries incurred in an internecine war.

So let the war between good and evil fight on inside each one of us, as indeed it does, and hopefully, if we become growingly aware of the need to defeat the evil within ourselves there will be growingly less warring between nation and nation outside ourselves, like the two Christian nations at war in Ireland where each group of citizens feel they're all right, and that the other group of citizens is all wrong.

I agree with F. Scott Peck's words in *People of the Lie: A Study of Human Evil* when he says that this war goes on inside almost all of us and that the few truly evil folks are those who have "lost the blessing of guilt," and they are the ones who often think they aren't bad at all, not at all, but that someone else sure as hell is, and they can punish that someone else without remorse and with impunity, and that when a nation they despise is filled with whomever they assume to be a generally evil people, unlike themselves, then it's let's raise the billions and billions of dollars it takes to bomb those people into burned and broken submission, and then billions and billions of dollars more to send in Bechtel and Halliburton to rebuild their roads and bridges, and we'll all get tons and tons of money, especially we weapons builders and international clean-up engineers, and to hell with the starving people and the orphans in the cities we've destroyed, and to hell with the schools and hospitals and help to other nations we might have spent that money on. Because the Kingdom of Heaven leads to life, but the Kingdom of Money leads to death, destruction, torment, and famine.

IT IS NOW QUITE out of fashion to think of Original Sin. But what else so well explains the deadly effects of mankind's aggregate presence on this planet? Holes appear in the ozone layer and the atmosphere thins out, making the sun a suddenly dangerous light source that now increasingly causes cancer. Plant and animal species that have taken the entire history of creation to produce are disappearing daily. The once teeming rivers and oceans have fewer and fewer life forms; the fish populations are diminishing as quickly as water on a griddle. Tigers, gorillas, all sorts of noble animals that once lived here in plentiful number, are suddenly finding themselves on the brink of extinction, and often caged for our pleasure, imprisoned and confined for our curiosity and amusement. Millions of people are starving when there is abundant food supply and the technical ability to distribute it. The leaders we elect are often lying cowards who preponderantly cater to the rich and powerful. The leaders we do not elect but who nevertheless inherit or seize their power are frequently despotic, cruel, and apparently heartless.

The presence of man on the planet Earth has been compared to a cancer: a presence that starts small in one spot, and then grows rapidly and spreads erratically and eats away, pollutes and destroys other living parts of the organism, man as a life-threatening and uniquely toxic part of creation.

Or perhaps we will blow all life away with our growing stockpiles of bombs and missiles. Or poison it with some pyrotechnic launching of anthrax or other hoarded evil treasure of killer microscopic bugs.

And this is the same mankind that produced Beethoven and Mozart and Brahms. That gets together and cooperates and works hard on producing an opera. That creates Peace Corps. That builds bridges. That learns how best to set bones and heal wounds. That feeds the hungry. That learns about solar energy and organic farming. That loves its neighbor, and husbands the Earth without greed or addiction, but rather reverence and wonder.

The war between good and evil goes on inside each one of us, but humanity in the aggregate, and humanity's effects on both our planet and the space that surrounds it are far from pretty, and closer to sickening. And the sickening results have no better explanation than that of our original sin, an explanation that, while no longer in fashion, fits the problem better than any other. Do you have a better, simpler, explanation? Pray tell me.

WHAT WAS YOUR ANSWER to that other, earlier, question, the one about whether you serve God—who is Love—or money? Remember, also, the familiar words that love of money is near the root of all evil.

I know when I see lots of money going into my wallet I feel something very close to love, if not love itself. I know I have more than two shirts and have not given away all but the one on my back to the man who has none. I know I arrive in church with more than two mites in my pocket, and that when the collection plate comes round I often give less than the amount that would hurt me to give.

I am not justified by works, but depend on God's mercy. If anything, unlike Peter Carota or Damien the Leper, Mother Teresa, or St. Francis, I am the rich man for whom entering the Kingdom of Heaven is more difficult than a camel's attempt to glide through the eye of a needle.

I do not visit or live in that Kingdom through my own worth and power.

My free invitation comes courtesy of an all-merciful God for whom all things are possible. Proper dress for guests at this wedding feast is gladness, adorned with heavy borders of gratitude.

THE UNITED STATES OF America is the current capital of the Kingdom of Money. The capital of this kingdom (a kingdom which growingly networks the globe) slowly moves from country to country and has formerly resided far from here, in ancient Rome, for example, or Spain or England. Some day it will move on from America, leaving us spent and hopefully wiser. Buying real estate in eastern or central Mongolia today might be a good investment for your grandchildren's financial future.

Because America is the country where money most triumphantly reigns now and is most venerated, because our government is willing to posture goodness while murdering and lying and practicing treachery on a large scale to protect and nurture its own economic interests and the economic interests of the rich few it really best serves, our way of talking and thinking about things has gradually changed during my lifetime, a lifetime which began in an economic depression brought about in America's first prolonged attempt to live and die by modern industry, big business, and the stock market.

In today's American language, money often is referred to as "the Bottom Line." We are very interested in the bottom line. We make decisions with only the bottom line in mind. We fire tens of thousands of factory workers without due notice in order to protect the bottom line. We poison the air and the people that breathe it because what's good for Monsanto and General Motors and Exxon and Dow Chemical is good for the country. Millions of our citizens sleep on the streets and go cold and hungry and are never mentioned in the platforms and speeches of both major parties' presidential election campaigns, and the presidential winner boasts of a booming economy, but who is it booming for? It is booming for the rich few that paid to elect him, and for the media moguls who fail to underline the sad fact that millions and millions of citizens work hard at full-time jobs yet cannot support their families, let alone rent a two-bedroom apartment to house them, or feed them without the help of food stamps.

When we say bottom line in America, I'm sorry to note we don't mean good will, or honesty, or integrity, or compassion. No, good will isn't our bottom line. Honesty isn't our bottom line. Integrity is not our bottom line. And compassion is most certainly not our bottom line. When we say bottom line in America, we mean only one thing, and the only thing we mean is money. And this figure of speech has only showed up in the last few decades, but the words and the priorities it symbolizes have hardened into common practice; we take them for granted, and we set our policies by them without any apparent conflict or remorse.

DANTE'S PICTURE OF HELL is the most prolonged and graphic picture of hell in the history of literature. His book, *Inferno*, begins with the narrator lost inside a dark forest with no point of reference from which to find his bearings, when he stumbles onto the Gates of Hell and enters through them.

He discovers that Hell itself is shaped rather like the inside of a vast and empty ice cream cone, and when he travels down Hell's spiraling trail each deeper level is inhabited by more of the damned humans who never repented of their sins, and the lower each level gets, the worse the sins of the damned are, and the more painful and tormenting their punishments

Finally, at the bottom of Hell, in the narrowest part of the ever-narrowing circle that the downward spiral through Hell provided, Dante comes upon a lake of solid ice, a lake with no water beneath the ice. Here is the deepest and worst spot in Hell, and there alone in its center, stuck up to his chest in the frozen solid water, the Devil is trapped and raging.

In the world of Dante's Hell, the Devil is the bottom line.

In Christ's words we can serve either God or Money, but not both.

The more we run after and clutch money, the more we make money our bottom line, the more we let go of God, the God of mercy, the God of compassion, and the God of truth.

Money is famous and covertly revered and worshiped for its mysterious ability to draw interest, but the interest it draws is ultimately illusory, the stuff of unreality and lies. Love of God draws the interest of truth. Who was it who said, "I am the Truth and the Way"?

5

Murder

Death is something you have wondered about, or celebrated, or mourned, or feared, or longed for from time to time throughout your life, and so it can be said in this sense you, the living, have accumulated some understanding, however limited, of death.

But the dead, no matter what you, the living, may think or feel about them, do not know death at all.

Either the dead have gone out of existence and are now no where, no how, and no thing, exactly as they were before they were born, or they've gone on into the next life still existing in one way or another, in which case they are still alive, and from their point of view, aren't dead at all, but hopefully more vital than ever.

We can be dying, and of course we all are; or we can die; but we can't be dead, except in the minds of the living.

If we die and know we did, then we aren't really dead, thank you. And if we die and truly cease to be, then we aren't experiencing death, either, except in the minds of the living.

But then no one knows, does one?

No one knows.

We only know that each one of us is dying.

Beyond this there is only betting on what happens or doesn't happen after the final fatal swallow of ocean water, the final sigh that follows the life-support system as it is rolled away, or the terminal shriek of the victim stabbed in the heart by a robber or an agent from the CIA.

I spoke with such an agent once. Was it CIA or some other branch of federal secret service? I can't remember, and now, with over twenty years gone by, the exact name of the bureaucratic division that licenses its employees to kill seems a relatively unimportant detail.

The poor fellow, who was quite handsome and athletic just as the James Bond movies have led us to expect, was in my office with his wife, and the two were trying marital therapy. As often happens in such undertakings, one spouse's individual issues surface because they've been contributing to the problems besetting the two of them.

This gentlemen's current complaint was the awful emotional pain he suffered when his usually suppressed recall of an assassination he had committed one dark night in Berlin during the Cold War came geysering back into his consciousness. He was sweating during the time he relived the incident in the presence of his wife and myself.

The detail I most remember was my client's tactile memory of his victim's heartbeating, rather a rapid fluttering beat, as I recall, a quick rhythm transmitted from the victim's suddenly traumatized heart along the penetrating knife blade and handle and from there into my client's right hand that expertly gripped that handle. I imagine the fast but rapidly dying vibrations traveled from my client's knife hand up his arm and most likely into his own heart, and the memory of this experience was helping to frustrate my client's attempts at intimacy with his own beloved.

Of course, one man in the story was dead at the time of the telling, a man my client had never encountered until the star-filled night he killed him, and the other man was alive and telling the tale for the two of them. But not in the urbane manner we have come to expect through the brave scriptwriters and actors who give us James Bond to help shape our socially acceptable views of murder for one's nation.

AND THEN A SIMILAR memory, this time about an executive who during one period of his life had flown on bombing missions over Vietnam. The executive's complaint was of an unexplainable anxiety he first experienced a few months prior to our first psychotherapy visit, and one that was growing in frequency and intensity, but with no apparent cause or pattern; the anxiety attacks always came without warning.

The history I took was unremarkable: my client had taken a routine climb up the American middle-class success ladder—the education, the job, the wife, the family, had all come into place neatly and in orderly fashion.

Only his war experience seemed at all extraordinary.

He had been the bombardier on a large warplane that repeatedly flew over Vietnam and dropped napalm bombs on villages, day after day, week after week, and month after month. All the missions had been routine and successful; he had never experienced any conscious guilt about his part in the matter, none at all, nor did he see why he should. (Once again I think of the movies, and the smiling pilots and the smiling thumbs-up the bombardiers give to the pilots, though because they are movies and meant to entertain us, there is usually enemy anti-aircraft flak and attacking fighter planes and an engine in flames on the port side before the tricky landing with one minor character hunched over dead in the tail gun section. Somehow this keeps mass murder from seeming too mundane, in the same sense that the murders of millions of people in the Nazi death camps were said to be experienced by the German soldiers as bureaucratic and mundane.)

My CIA client, who as far as I know had only murdered one person, and that in a manner that was up-close and personal, at least knew what was bothering him, and that is a leg up on solving any psychological problem. The executive who had pulled the trigger that unleashed the destruction of hundreds of towns and villages, the horrible burning of thousands of grownups and children, and the killing of perhaps tens of thousands of people had no idea what was causing his anxiety and suffering, and he rejected both me and my far-out speculations.

When the Air Force told him he had spent enough time dropping napalm to suit them he went home and resumed his pleasant life. He seldom if ever thought about his wartime days. He was surprised and resistant to my asking him to talk and think about those days now. He disagreed with my belief that the knowledge he had pulled the trigger that launched the deaths and suffering of so many people was at all troubling to him, or ever had been. He insisted that he had felt nothing because he had seen nothing. Nothing but the radar screen on his bombsight: a black, white, and gray screen, smaller than a television set, with grids and numbers and a button for a napalm bomb trigger.

The executive disliked my theories about his emotional denial, and after a few interviews, called to cancel his appointment and said he'd be seeking help elsewhere. Anxiety. A bio-chemical imbalance. Perhaps the right medication to set his neuro-chemistry back on track. Thousands dead, one man living. A respectable patriot, a good Joe, but suffering from an anxiety with no apparent cause.

I REMEMBER WORKING AS a psychotherapist for a county mental health agency during the Vietnam war. Although my hours were primarily spent in the outpatient clinic, I also screened and admitted people to the inpatient ward, also known as the neuro-psychiatric hospital, the insane asylum, or the crazy house, and I often visited that ward and its patients for routine follow-up. One day I came across a poem that one of the inmates had written, a lady I later found out had been committed to the locked ward by due process of law. *Gentle Jesus, bless each bomb.*

At the time the line struck me as starkly sane. These were the days when criticisms of the war were branded unpatriotic, erroneous, suspect, and dangerous. During these days the television reporters would interview soldiers at the front and present their sound bites on each day's evening news. The interviewed soldiers invariably spoke well of the war, and of the rightness and gladness they felt at maiming people, killing people, and risking their own lives to keep the world safe for democracy (read capitalism). If there were any soldiers who fought, killed, wounded, or were wounded there that felt otherwise, the news broadcasts never reported their thoughts and feelings. Any heartfelt and strong criticism of the war was considered subversive, misguided, or downright evil—isn't Jane Fonda spending the rest of her life trying to live this one down? A simple, apt dismissal of the morality of the whole misguided endeavor could only be found in the poetry of someone put away as legally crazy.

When someone else does the murdering, our cameras are there. If a Middle Eastern despot has poison-gassed some of his citizenry, we'll record each corpse's gaping mouth and stiffened grasping hand and show the grotesque bodies lying in rows out on the village street for every evening news, and then we'll show it all again each time we're ready to justify another multi-billion-dollar military campaign against said despot, or another one like him.

But as a rule we are not much for showing the carnage we Americans cause. Weren't there some wondrously burned bodies somewhere in Grenada, and whatever became of their pictures? Didn't we murder thousands of civilians (the same sort of civilians that you, I, our mothers and children are) during our war in Panama? I never saw or heard a reporter holding a microphone over their bodies, did you? There were stories of hundreds, if not thousands, of Iraqi soldiers being bulldozed alive in their bunkers, and then drowning beneath the sand like torpedoed sailors once drowned in water, but where were our news cameras? And why not equal time for all the other burned, buried, and exploded victims of American diplomacy, the special version of diplomacy that is usually reserved for the nations with a darker-skinned citizenry.

The official sanity does not write the kind of good poetry that might only be found on a wartime psych ward; it writes bad poetry, and gives wars titles like Operation Desert Storm and Operation Just Cause. Unlike the word *operation* with its connotations of painful risk for a healthy outcome, the word *war* implies mass murder. And war's machinery, from the days of the sword, and boiling oil poured from castle battlements, to the current time of jet aircraft and expensive computer driven smart weaponry, is always designed to kill and destroy our brothers, our fellow man. But of late the talented bureaucrats in our government's marketing department, the folks who are paid to sell us on the goodness and rightness of any current killing endeavor, are using the same linguistic style we used to reserve for naming a new perfume.

GOD IS A MUCH simpler prose stylist than most of us. He doesn't write often, usually preferring to jot down ideas and admonitions through guys we call prophets, like Isaiah or Jeremiah, but then once in a while he bypasses the middleman and inscribes words himself, maybe on something more stable than paper, something like stone.

Take the day he inscribed his final draft of the Ten Commandments on the tablets Moses was carrying. God was instructing us living people on how to play the game of life. Stay inside these rules and you're a varsity member of the winning team.

The rules are quite simple, every bit as simple as the baseball rule that if you catch his fly ball the batter is out.

Okay. The batter hits an awesome towering drive that rockets over the infield and all the way back to the rear of the warning track. It is just a wonderful hit, and only a star athlete could have smacked it that far, yet the center fielder catches the ball before it touches anything but his fielding mitt. The batter is out. No one ever disputes that.

So God comes up with ten rules. And one of them is simpler by far than the simple baseball rule I just quoted, and God's simple rule is: Thou Shall Not Kill.

I don't know of anywhere in the world where grown men or grown women are catching fly balls during a baseball game and the batter is still being allowed to advance to first base after his hit was caught. It just never happens, even though a lot of teams, especially losing ones, would like to bypass that rule a few times to get back on top, or at least into a more competitive position.

But now, Thou Shall Not Kill. That's harder to follow. Maybe God didn't mean what he said the time he wrote it on some stone tablets Moses was carrying on top of a mountain that was covered with smoke and fire and Moses came down the mountain later with his face bathed in white light and carrying the tablets, and one of the few things God had written on the tablets was Thou Shall Not Kill. But maybe God didn't really mean it, and that's why he gave us those rules in such a casual and undramatic manner.

But the Bible contradicts itself on this matter, as it so often does on many other matters, and also reports God saying a man who abducts someone shall be put to death, a man who strikes his mother or father shall be put to death, a man who plans and carries out the violent death of another shall be put to death, and a man who curses his mother shall be put to death. Well, someone is going to have to put each of these offenders to death, and how can they execute them for capital crimes when God, "with his own finger," wrote, Thou Shall Not Kill on two stone tablets, and made Thou Shall Not Kill one of his top ten laws?

The Jewish people after Moses's time responded to this conundrum by voting in favor of the more complicated side of this legal question, and they then wrote yet more laws about killing people for perfectly legal reasons. That seems to be the response of their leadership to the issue of what to do with the Fifth Commandment. In fact they made up laws on damn near everything. They had laws upon laws, and laws about laws, just like we do, and goodness was often defined by how well you followed the laws, and this was a very time-consuming thing and took an excellent memory, like remembering to send your wife to a special building when she was having her period, although she would have the company of all the other currently menstruating ladies.

Then along came Jesus. And Jesus boiled all these laws down to two easy to remember commandments: First, you had to love God with everything you had, your whole heart, your whole mind, and your whole soul. And second, you had to love your neighbor as yourself.

Sounds simple, but in some ways Jesus's simplifying of all the laws reads more like a Zen koan, a mind-blower, because if you're spending all the love you have, every bit of it, on loving God, how do you have any love left over to love yourself and your neighbor?

One solution, the one a number of thinkers and theologians have come up with, is that you *are* God and so is your neighbor; at least the two of you are essentially God, even though both of you have some non-God crud, or bad parts, or sins, accruing to you. This view would fit with Jesus's statement that he and the Father are one, but that the Father is greater than him, and that all the things that were true of him were true of us as well, especially true if we happened to hear and believe what he was saying, but maybe even true for the unbeliever. This second reality, that we are essentially like Jesus, one in Jesus, adopted children of God and therefore one with God, is heralded in various ways throughout the New Testament by both Jesus and his disciples. But if this is too far-fetched for you perhaps you can come up with a better answer to the question of harmonizing the two commandments of Jesus: love God with all the love you have, but still have enough love left over to love your neighbor as yourself.

NOW BACK TO THE subject of death or murder. Remember the Gospel account of the woman discovered in adultery, and all the law-abiding men getting ready to kill her by stoning her to death? They were simply believers in capital punishment for a capital crime. And Jesus shows up and gets down on his haunches and draws his finger in the sand a while, kind of reminiscent of God drawing his finger across the stone tablets and writing laws for Moses to carry down the mountain, and then Jesus looks up and says, "Let he who has not sinned cast the first stone." And all the law-abiding exponents of capital punishment just kind of shuffle off in silence.

In an earlier section of this book I talked about how the language Jesus uses is inclusive, and that a word like "neighbor" probably means more than just the folks who live in the houses on either side of your house. With that in mind, we may be learning more than just how Jesus reacted in this one situation. We might be learning that Jesus is talking about (among other things) capital punishment in general. Let he who has not sinned drop the first guillotine blade, spring the first hangman's trap, pull the first electric chair switch, fire the first firing squad bullet, drop the first cyanide pellet, stick the first lethal injection in their fellow man's arm. Or was he just talking about adulteresses and not to stone them to death unless you are the exceptional man who has never thought of cheating on your wife?

He said if we lust in our heart we're as guilty as that condemned adulteress was. Does this kind of guilt begin and end with adultery and our fantasies about it? Or does it apply to wishing someone were dead, or thinking about murdering someone in one of our daydreams? If you've done either of those things perhaps you've lost your right to legally murder your brothers and sisters, to cast the first stone.

Capital punishment: a legal way to murder. But it seems to go against the commandment of loving your neighbor as yourself at all times, unless you are sure that you are one of those brave few who would gladly lie down on a gurney for a justly lethal injection and never wish for mercy. And unless you've never murdered in your heart.

I WAS HONORED BY my peers once. I got asked to speak at all four Sunday masses at our parish church on behalf of the Respect Life Commission, a church group that was formed to dissuade and enlighten those who might otherwise think favorably of abortion, abortion often being seen as a violation

of the commandment, Thou Shall Not Kill. Part of my required prepara-
tion for the talk would be to attend a Saturday instructional meeting with
a group of other folks who were also so honored, one honored person for
every parish church in the diocese. We would be taught what was expected
from us when we stood before our congregations, spoke to them, and perhaps were asked questions by them.

I showed up at the meeting, which was led by a young well-credentialed
public relations lady who was wearing expensive clothing and looked like a
candidate for television news anchor on the evening news. I remember she
made a special and prolonged point of telling us what an innovator Richard
Nixon had been when it came to dealing with hostile questions from an
audience, be they reporters or voters or fellow politicians.

Nixon's basic strategy, which was a new one at the time, was to appear
to listen carefully to the question, and if it was either hostile or not to his
liking, then to answer as if he'd been asked an altogether different question,
a question that he, Nixon, had in fact made up in his own mind, and do all
this with a straight face and proper voice tones, acting exactly as if he was
being candid and straightforward.

"Mr. President, how do you respond to reports that you are currently
bombing Cambodia?"

"Thank you Jack. Our forces, as you know, are the finest military forces
in the world today. They are ready to deploy at a moment's notice, to focus
immense striking power wherever the safety and protection of our nation
requires. The men that man our weaponry are beyond question the finest
and most loyal fighters the world has ever known, and their excellence and
integrity are an example that is worthy of every loyal American's respect and
admiration . . . Miranda. You had a question."

Our guest trainer loved and admired this style of Nixonian strategy and
taught us how to do it ourselves, and thoroughly. Many of the honored
Respect Life Commission speakers seemed to take in this lesson like something out of the Gospels, even though it was in reality a recipe cooked up
by a master of lying and deception, and all this happened under the auspice
of the Catholic Church.

This was one of the methods we were to use in our fight to protect the unborn, a better strategy than killing a doctor who performs abortions, a better strategy than bombing an abortion clinic, but still on the wrong side of the scale that weighs out virtue and vice. It was part of the old tired view that an evil method is somehow justified by an end that is believed to be virtuous.

As the day wore on some of the students in this prep class asked about Respect Life issues as they pertained to war and capital punishment. One of the men who was putting on the seminar stood up and delivered a prolonged and impassioned defense of both killing folks in a war and killing condemned criminals. Later that afternoon I resigned my commission as a Respect Life Commission speaker and was never invited for another tryout.

Is abortion murder? I don't know, do you? I wouldn't do it; at least I don't think I would. A priest told me once that St. Thomas Aquinas said the embryo didn't have a soul until it was three months old. And there are those who argue that life begins when we take our first breath and not before, and have biblical quotes to support their theory. Maybe some scholar could check these views out further.

There are also the other considerations, like judge not lest you be judged. Don't busy yourself too much locating the speck in your neighbor's eye and missing the beam in your own. And so on.

A young unmarried couple I knew long ago discovered that they were pregnant. The boyfriend was in favor of getting married and having the baby, but the young lady said no, and not to worry, she had already had five prior abortions. Piece of cake, she implied. She had her way, and the two of them made an afternoon appointment with her trusty abortion doctor. Nice homey office with color photographs on the coffee table of the surgeon standing beside his racecar collection. The young father stayed in the waiting room, and in a while the young lady came out, smiling. And all this was years before abortions were legal.

This highly fertile but unwilling woman seemed sunny by nature and took her latest venture in stride. The young man felt guilty, but he chalked it off to his lack of adult savoir-faire.

A few years later they married, and a year after the wedding she gave birth to their first child, a son. The infant was born with a blood problem of unknown etiology: his skin yellowed deeply and he quickly and increasingly weakened. After a day or two the doctors told the new parents that their child required a complete blood exchange in order to survive, and that this procedure had a slight risk, but only one chance in a hundred, of proving fatal.

The day and night before the blood exchange the baby's father felt stressed and fearful, but the baby's mother fell apart completely, finally locking herself in the bathroom for hours where she could wail and wring her hands in a self-imposed solitary confinement. When she at last emerged, it was to shout out that she was being punished for the six abortions she had so blithely undergone. She was all but completely certain that her firstborn would die on the blood exchange table (he didn't). All that guilt, which she had so artfully and sunnily buried under her conscious awareness, had come bursting up to torture her and punish her with a dreadful despair.

So far I've been talking about murder, and how murderers feel about their deadly deeds. The dictionary says murder is the crime of killing someone unlawfully, and all right, I buy that definition, but whose set of laws are we talking about? For a number of years the novelist Salmon Rushdie could have been killed by a Muslim assassin, and though many people would have thought it was murder, many others would have seen his death as a casualty of war, just like we Americans tend to look at the murders of mothers and children we committed during the war in Bosnia as something other than murders, and use the language of psychological denial: "The Bosnians suffered casualties during allied bombing." Or worse yet, "The Bosnians suffered collateral damage."

If you ever have to run home from work after the bombers have flown by so high in the sky you couldn't see them, and then feel impelled to clear away some of the rubble your home made when it exploded, if, half buried beneath the debris, you spot the hand of your wife or the foot of the child you kissed goodbye earlier that morning, and you trace their limbs to their now dead bodies, you will feel much the same as you would had they died at the hand of any murderer, however common. The fact that in someone's book of rules the deaths were declared lawful will fail to console you.

In the law books of many of the nations of the world it is legal to kill your fellow human, and it is again interesting to remember that it was just such a law book that justified the legal murder of Jesus by Pilate. In some ways Jesus was a casualty of war, too, because the Roman armies that crucified him had conquered Israel and were occupying it during the poor man's lifetime, I suppose under some justification like New World Order, the language lately popularized by American presidencies.

The fact is that the citizens of ancient Rome, and the citizens of its surrounding Italian villages, had to pay no taxes at that time, no taxes at all. The money they needed to run their expensive government and to enrich their kingly caesars and wealthy senators and generals came from the heavy tariffs they levied upon sixteen countries or provinces their Legions had speared and stabbed into submission the way we now bomb and tank countries into submission. They did this largely under the guise of bringing Roman civilization to otherwise benighted barbarians, but actually the Romans were occupying Israel for economic reasons, which is why tax collectors are often alluded to in the Gospels as undesirable social outcasts.

The New World Order Rome was enforcing in Israel was kinder to the Jewish aristocrats than to the Jewish common man, and of course Jesus was not only a common man by birth and social station, but a great leader and leveler, the great equalizer, the great lover of every man, and true love does not know condescension. In short, he was a formidable enemy of the hierarchical power structure, both religious and political, and this was exactly the sort of power structure that invariably rules by the prison, the sword, the cross, the smart bomb, or the electric chair. Not murder, you know, just a bit of civilized killing for the sake of nurturing law and order.

BUT HERE'S A RUB: if Jesus is really God, and somehow equal to God the Father, then there's a certain suicidality to his having been killed at the hands of the secular and religious governments. After all, God knew all along what was going to happen to his son, and how his son was going to die, and if Jesus is one in being with the Father, and if Jesus is the eternal Word, the Logos that has lived outside of creation as long as the Father has been around, then Jesus was in on how his earthly life would end long before he came sliding out of the Virgin's tunnel of love.

My catechism teacher explained to me that God didn't need suffering and the crucifixion and murdering of his son to save us. He could have saved us any way he pleased to, maybe by making a particular tree grow, or dividing the moon in two, or just snapping his fingers once. Why he chose to do it the way he did, and why he chose to do it at all, is a mystery, as is the rest of the creation, though God's great love for the world has been said to have something to do with it.

But the suicidal element in Jesus's life plan has always intrigued me: suicide with some greater purpose in mind, like a World War II kamikaze fighter pilot crashing his plane into a battleship for the glory of Japan, or an Arab disintegrating from the discharge of dynamite he had belted round his midriff for Allah and the downfall of Israel.

Although, as I mentioned earlier, the suicide mission Jesus was on was for the ultimate welfare of everybody.

My own father killed himself at the age of thirty-two, and our milkman discovered his body, which was hanging by the neck from a rope tied around a pipe in the underpart of the apartment house our family lived in at the time. My mother was twenty-seven, my brother almost five, and I was a few months under two.

My father had been a decent and loving man who worked three jobs to make ends meet in Chicago during the Great Depression. By day he was liquor buyer for a department store named Weibolts. At night he washed the grimy windows of the old elevated train cars as they rested in their storage barns. Part of each weekend he served as a youth leader for the YMCA.

I don't really know why he killed himself, although I've done a good deal of investigating and have lots of theories. Also the nature of his death has given me a deep and intense interest in suicide, both in those who do it and those who come close and like to frequently visit its borders.

Of course dealing with suicide and suicidal risk are part of most psychotherapists' yearly staple, and for those therapists who work with the severely disturbed and psychotic, the sort of patients who are regularly hospitalized and on powerful emotion-numbing drugs, the suicide of at least someone in their caseload can become all-too familiar.

I have also known from my own experience what it's like to have prolonged suicidal urges and ideation, urges that lasted for up to half a year at
a time. I have had my head inside of unlit gas-filled ovens and then backed
out of them, and I have sold my rifle to a gun shop just to get the deadly
temptation out of my home.

I sweated out clients' suicidal threats with some frequency and listened
in staff meetings when other therapists mourned the loss of someone whose
life they had failed to save, and I believe suicide is a great mystery, in part
because it is so much like murder.

One theory goes that if you are close to killing yourself then you are also
close to killing someone else, and you may have noticed how frequently
someone kills anywhere from one to ten people on some sunny day, and
then he (it is almost always a he) turns the gun to his own head.

Murder and suicide are getting to be such popular forms of dying in
our culture that we now have suicide hot lines and if you feel the urge to
kill yourself you can telephone and speak with someone intent on talking
you into going on living.

During my lifetime, four people I was close to have killed themselves.
One hanged himself. The other three died of self-inflicted gun wounds.
Two were men and two were women. And all four were very nice people.

And yet there is this fairly common attitude that suicide is the most
damnable of crimes. People tend to envision Judas Iscariot in Hell, and
part of their belief stems from the view that he killed himself, and that it
was killing himself, rather than his fingering Jesus to the authorities, that
constituted the unforgivable sin.

Try reading Jorge Luis Borges's essay, "Three Versions of Judas." Borges
was a blind Argentine poet and writer whom many thought was unfairly—
because he wrote so much and so well—passed over for a Nobel Prize. In
his essay on Judas, Borges puts forth the case that Judas, not Jesus, was the
real Messiah, and he uses scripture to back up his arguments.

One plea that might be used to argue for the element of innocence found
in all suicides could be based on the hundreds of infants who decided to
starve themselves to death during the London Blitz. German bombs and
rockets had orphaned so many babies that the English government had to

set up state-run nurseries, and there the newborns lay in long orderly rows of tiny cribs, with efficient English nurses working hard to see to it that the babies' diapers and bedding were regularly changed and that feedings took place right on schedule.

To everyone's surprise and bafflement, a shockingly large percentage of the babies stopped eating and began wasting away and finally died. The fatal behavior grew so common that the English used a somewhat esoteric word for their condition, *marasmus*, or fatal failure to thrive due to malnutrition. This growing movement in group suicide stopped when someone discovered that holding, cuddling, or, in short, loving the babies for a couple of twenty minute periods a day ended the little people's exercise in self-destruction.

I want to both honor the mystery in a successful suicide, and to never ever take lightly even the tiniest hints some folks give that they are thinking about murdering themselves. With that in mind, let's note that some babies suicide when they don't feel loved. Too young, too weak, and too uncoordinated to pick up a gun or take pills or connect a hose to the exhaust pipe, they simply refuse food and starve themselves to death. But if they feel loved, in time they willingly give up their lethal behavior.

I believe the same might often be said of the adult population, that feeling painfully unloved or unlovable, especially when combined with the despair that comes from being blind to any way out of the ensuing anguish, can make even a fearsome death seem like the lesser of two evils, and offers the remote chance of welcome relief.

I remember doing family therapy with a forty-year-old single man as the patient. He was suffering from paranoid schizophrenia and was not always the best of company. His father was dead, but his mother, older brother, and younger sister were all present for the therapy sessions. During one meeting the young man talked about wanting to kill himself, and I asked each family member in turn how he or she would feel if he carried out his threat. Mother, sister, brother all said in so many words that their lives would probably be considerably better with him out of it. At the time I was shocked, but in retrospect it was good to get these underlying feelings, that I'm sure were affecting the designated patient adversely, out into the light and visible, rather than working their dark magic beneath an ocean of malignant silence.

And the many people who, like Sigmund Freud, kill themselves because the pain of their physical illness is greater than they can, or wish to, bear: their deaths may be mercy killings. They are often abetted by the doctors who see to it that the sufferers have enough morphine or other potentially lethal substance to take them to what they hope is a better place, because any place seems preferable to the torment that hopelessly envelops them.

I remember one of the dearest and most devout Christian women I have ever met, consumed with cancer that wasted her body to corpse-like proportions and invaded her every cell with knifing pain, and she finally could take no more of it, but her doctor, who also called himself a Christian, withheld a lethal amount of painkillers from her on the grounds that killing herself would be a sin. The woman's distraught husband, also an ardent Christian, had to look up a local doctor who did not believe in the afterlife, and got from him the necessary dosage and then sat holding his wife's hand and caressing her as she passed away.

The suicides that are committed to escape unbearable physical pain are the easiest for the loved one's survivors. Those suicides committed to escape psychological pain are the hardest and most wounding for those the dead leave behind. If you are contemplating suicide and have people who love you in your life, children for example, just say no. If you possibly can. Bear your suffering for their sake, as Jesus bore his suffering for ours.

Now I AM GOING to date myself and talk about a sex murder that took place in the mid-twentieth century in Los Angeles. The press christened it "The Black Dahlia Murder" and the story stayed in the newspapers darn near forever. Here's what I remember, and I may be getting part of it wrong, but here goes anyway: A woman in her early twenties was found murdered, her naked and mutilated body discovered in a vacant lot. She had long black hair, was beautiful, had aspired to Hollywood stardom, and always wore fashionable black clothes to complement her slender and splendid figure. Some news reporter called her the Black Dahlia and everyone in town, and the nation for all I know, had something to think about and get excited over.

I believe I was twelve years old at the time and, without anyone telling me to, I discovered how exciting sex combined with murder can be.

In retrospect, those were innocent days. Now we are chock full of such murders and our sensibilities are rather inured to them. Ted Bundy is yesterday's news, and he had to kill many more than one woman to become infamous. But Ted helped popularize the serial killing trend (unless you count wars), and now the rule is that usually a man must kill more than several people to take center stage in the media.

There are exceptions. The O. J. Simpson trial in the 1990s, when I was writing the first drafts of this book, involved the deaths of only two people, although sex certainly played a central part in the public's appetite for gobs of information about the case. And O. J.'s story also paralleled the play *Othello*, where a locally famous black general has crossed the color line for a blonde, and jealousy motivates his murderous rage. In the real-life version of this drama, although we can only suspect who the actual murderer is, the events still read a lot like Shakespeare's play, but with a sixth act called The Trial thrown in for good measure.

And there was the JonBenét Ramsey Case, where only one person was murdered, but with grotesquely perverted sex involved, and this grotesquely perverted sex is a current major trend in newsworthy murders, with Jeffrey Dahmer, a serial murderer who embodied numerous perversions, being the high-point trendsetter in the last quarter of the twentieth century. We are so fascinated with such cruel and deadly behaviors that we make arch movies about them and give the actors in these films Academy Awards. When actor Anthony Hopkins was interviewed on the *Today Show*, he and Katie Couric laughed together at his reprise of the fictional Hannibal Lector's deliberate habit, in *The Silence of the The Lambs*, of sucking in his own saliva when he speaks of the special taste of a recent victim's flesh.

In an earlier, quieter time we laughed at Cary Grant's confusion when confronted with growing evidence that his two sweet and eccentric maiden aunts were fatally poisoning their elderly gentleman callers. A modern *Arsenic and Old Lace* might have these old dearies strangling and stabbing their victims first, and then barbecuing their genitals on a spit.

A while back a man in South America was discovered having tortured and murdered some one hundred forty boys, and this made the American newspapers, but more largely on the back pages, and the story rapidly lost steam because after all, they were "not our boys," and "not one of ours." This ethnocentric attitude also surfaces with war casualties, where thousands of murdered Panamanians, Haitians, Bosnians, Grenadians, Iraqis, Syrians, Sudanese, etc., are not one of ours, not one of our boys, and therefore hardly worth the mention. But when only one or three of our boys dies, or is badly beaten up by the enemy, the nation mourns and wrings its fingers in anguish. Very different from St. Paul's view that there is "neither Jew nor Greek . . . but we are all one in Jesus Christ." And this from a nation that often calls itself Christian.

By the way, the man who murdered one hundred forty boys spent much of his own childhood being brutally beaten by his father and repeatedly raped by two neighbors. All people so treated do not grow up to be serial murderers, but ninety-nine percent of the people who do murder have extremely disturbing factors present during their formative years, something our nation's economists might include in their spreadsheets when deciding how much to spend on mental health funds and how much on prisons.

I once worked with a very troubled young gentleman who wanted to be a Buddhist monk and a man of peace, but found himself cycling in and out of state mental hospitals instead. His father was outraged with his son for letting his hair grow long. This was in the early 1970s when long hair and beards were still capable of striking fire in the hearts of less adventuresome spirits. Because this psychotic young man (let's call him Bill) was flat-out poor and probably unemployable at the time, he could only afford the services of our county mental health facilities, and that was where I was working.

Bill liked me very much as a therapist, but I couldn't see him individually because the state hadn't allocated the funds to make that possible, so I saw him almost exclusively in group therapy until he once again reentered the state mental hospital.

Upon his release from the hospital, Bill asked to see me again, but our county's criminally low mental health budget made that impossible as I had already been jammed to the gills in his brief absence and was overflowing with patient hours, and so Bill was transferred to someone else, in the routine and bureaucratic manner of mental health facilities for the poor.

In later years Bill got some of the personal attention he needed by kill-ing nine people, doing so on the convincing instruction of voices he heard that no one else heard. Bill's room and board at the state prison in which he currently resides costs taxpayers in the neighborhood of $60,000 a year. That would pay for a lot of individual psychotherapy hours.

BUT I'M BEGINNING TO get sick of talking about murder and you are prob-ably beginning to get sick of hearing about it, although getting sick or sated with talk of murder might be a good thing as our culture has been grow-ingly and steadfastly absorbed with murder, perhaps in a way addicted to it, and it might be nice if we found the deed less fascinating and attractive, don't you think?

So I will try to finish with this topic as soon as possible, but there is a rapidly growing strain of murder I want to mention first, and that's the sort of murder undertaken by the man or boy who stocks up his basement, garage or bedroom with military weaponry, puts on his camouflaged fatigues and combat boots and opens fire on the civilian inhabitants of a factory, post office, schoolyard, or synagogue, or plants a mega-bomb in a large building, sometimes for some belief he has and sometimes just for the ornery thrill of it.

Television likes to show our professional pundits sitting around in small serious groups pondering the causes of this ever-growing lethal epidemic. The journalistic sages appear to be thinking and theorizing deeply, and week by week go over every possibility they can imagine that might explain this new mystery to them. When another schoolboy opens automatic weapons fire on his classmates in the cafeteria, or when a clean-cut lad in his twenties bombs the life out of hundreds in a federal office building, then television cameras move in for tight shots of these very well-dressed affluent men and women who are paid millions of dollars to gather in a circle of armchairs and offer professional explanations for the sure signs that there is something going growingly wrong in America. But there are two pieces of data I never hear them consider, and I will return to these two obvious omissions in a moment.

First I want to mention a couple more murderers I worked with after they had committed their deadly crimes, because there is something about both of them that I think throws light on the causes that seem to have our journalists stumped.

I saw both men under the budget constraints of county mental health, which is to say that, as was the case with Bill, I saw them almost entirely in group therapy, with perhaps two or three individual sessions each in a year. Neither man knew nor ever met the other during the time I worked with them.

Both men were in their sixties. Both had killed their wives twenty or thirty years before, had gone to prison, served time, and been released. Both were currently working as barbers in small rather rundown barbershops. Both lived alone in small studio apartments. Neither had a pet. Neither had any sort of developed social network or friendships. Neither went out much, if at all, to social events or entertainments, including movies. Both were affectless and taciturn in group. Both were attending psychotherapy as a condition of parole.

It gradually dawned on me that both men were unconsciously keeping themselves imprisoned, that both were living out their own sparse civilian version of lifetime solitary confinement, as close a version as they could come up with under their current circumstances. And both men were very clinically depressed. In a word, both were self-punishing.

THE TWO GROUPS OF data our professional news analysts never mention that I feel are begging to be looked at, are:

First, the mass murderers, both the old-fashioned stalk-and-kill-one-victim-at-a-time kind (who can take years to complete their lengthy list of fatal casualties), and the newer more efficient get-out-your-advanced-military-weaponry-and-wipe-out-as-many-lives-as-you-can-all-at-once kind, are almost entirely drawn from the ranks of our native-born white male Protestant middle class.

If the predominant killer group were otherwise, say a small but growing corps of killers largely made up of Jews (may God forbid), or blacks or Hispanics, or even more unusual, a growing group of women who pulled the triggers before or after molesting their victims or dynamiting the pre-school,

Chris Matthews and his lookalikes would be rubbing their jaws and making much of it, puzzling deeply about its social meaning and implications for government action. But when the killers come from the legions of America's most privileged and catered-to social class, the network sages go blind to that obvious in-your-face pattern and therefore incapable of mentioning it.

And the second piece of constantly overlooked data is just as troubling. The circle of network experts and op-ed writers are all searching for a cause for the upsurge in citizens bearing arms against, well, their fellow citizens. All possibilities are given the appearance of being carefully examined: Could it be the violence in movies? The violence in television? Could it be the violence in video games? In comic books? Are parents not spending enough time with their children? Is public education in some way failing us? Perhaps, say the pundits, it could be all of these, or some sub-group of these. Well, we have thought seriously and deeply of everything we can think of, we have informed our viewers with the fruits of our exhaustive ponderings. It is time to go home now and loosen our $300 neckties. We have done our best.

What they always fail to mention or allude to is our government's own continued and growing addiction to putting on military camouflage, loading up the family plane with automatic weapons and explosives and then trotting itself off to do right for the world by bombing or machine-gunning a sizeable portion, usually a dark-skinned portion, of the world's citizenry.

These images, too, have been before us as long as most of us have been alive, portrayed in the stirring terms supplied by the films our Defense Department ships to the media: Ronald Reagan wearing his military costume peering through his military binoculars at the North Korean defense emplacements. Attractive and earnest young American soldiers standing tall on the sands of Iraq. Operation Just Cause. How exhilarating and chest-pumpingly patriotic it all is for us.

Forget the murders involved. Bury them deeply in the national subconscious. Keep the denial going with the help of spin-doctor media experts who soothe you on the topic of possible causes for schoolyard shootings. Experts who are paid millions of dollars by the billion-dollar media industries who employ them, industries both owned and sponsored by corporations that make more money than you've ever dreamed of every time we murder lots more folks in some far-off land.

BUT MURDER WILL OUT: The CIA agent can't get close to his wife. The executive feels painfully anxious from unknown causes. The blithe recipient of abortions falls apart when her buried guilt comes rising from its tomb alive and fully vengeful. The paroled barbers remain self-imprisoned. Not to mention all the veterans who can't see a war movie or read a war book without losing sleep for weeks to the recurring nightmares that awaken them. You can only ignore or rationalize guilt for so long, and then it will turn around and bite you painfully, sometimes murderously.

In family therapy we have the concept of Symptom Bearer. The symptom bearer is usually the family scapegoat as well; the person whom other family members feel is making things bad in the family, and that if only the symptom bearer was different everything in the family would be hunky-dory.

Therapists long ago discovered that the symptom bearer is not only himself or herself a sick puppy, but a sign that something is quite wrong and unhealthy in the entire family system as well, which is to say, in all of the family members.

I saw an apparently happy middle-class family in therapy once because the family symptom bearer and scapegoat was a pretty fourteen-year-old girl who was angry and running away from home a lot and therefore seen by other family members as the sole fly in their otherwise spotless ointment. In the first session, which also included both parents, her two sisters and a brother, the girl was verbally attacked by her mother who launched into an explosion of hot railing that was aimed directly at her and her adolescent misbehavior.

"Don't you think I'd just like to just run away!!! Don't you think at times I'd just like to drop the dish towel and walk out the door and never come back!!"

And on and on mother went. But mother didn't really realize what she was saying by implication, or that daughter was probably acting out mother's own usually unspeakable and perhaps unconscious discontent over a life that appeared happy on the surface while in fact being filled too high with chronic frustration.

I think America is like that family in some ways. The smooth-jawed smiling clean-cut white man, usually a Protestant, that Ronald Reagan, George Bush I, Bill Clinton, and George Bush II so ably represented (though we know the act in many ways was just an act, like the mask of contentment the mother in family therapy wore), those affable well-coifed fellows all signed papers that decreed thousands of people would be murdered, though they used soft lying words like "some civilian casualties," and that the rest of us were just to keep on smiling, stand up for the "Star Spangled Banner" at the start of ball games, and proudly wear our red, white, and blue good conduct medals pinned above our hearts.

But murder will out. And the bombsight trigger has perhaps been punched once too often. And Hell is beginning to break out here.

As he left the presidency, Dwight Eisenhower said the biggest danger facing America was the Military-Industrial Complex. He didn't call our greatest danger the Communist menace. Or the Vietnamese. Or the Cambodians. Or the people of Grenada, Haiti, Iraq, or Iran. Or Manuel Noriega or Saddam Hussein or Bashar Assad. The great danger Ike cited was a danger inside our own borders, a part of our own social fabric, a part of our own family, owned and operated by our own citizens, our own family members.

That Military-Industrial Complex, murder for hire, is rather well camouflaged itself considering its vast size, its ever-growing vast size; and its awesome level of economic activity and profit has not only gobbled up a lion's share of our taxes, but a lion's share of the taxes of almost every one of the countries we've fought. Those countries usually use the arms our weapons industries have sold them, just before the war begins.

I believe the new wave of senseless instantaneous mass murder of innocent white middle-class victims that is being carried out by white middle-class Protestant males mimics and calls attention to the continued evil and wickedness of our polite and polished Federal Government, and its well-worn policies of making every citizen work hard and long for the welfare of our cleverly camouflaged Jabba the Hutt tax-eating, soul-injuring Military-Industrial Complex.

After all, Rambo was only the captivatingly dramatic embodiment of our nation's patriotic flair for murdering foreign folks in droves. The real kids these days who strap on bandoliers and drop large parts of their school population in bloody heaps outside the auditorium are basically imitating Dad the President, rather than Sylvester Stallone.

But it just isn't fashionable to speak this truth. Isn't done. Must be the video games. We love the emperor's clothes.

WE ARE SO VERY much like the Rome of Gospel days: International ass-kicker, our troops stationed here, there, damn near everywhere, tropic islands, desert sands, European cities. We are present, guns at the ready, to make the world safe for democracy, or so we say. Bullets, bombs and rockets, civilian corpses and amputees have seldom multiplied as quickly as since the Berlin Wall came down, and capitalism—also known as money—vanquished the economic system Ronald Reagan called the Evil Empire.

So it is democratic law and order, or so the networks tell us. Actually our citizenry's wishes as measured by pollsters were completely ignored in most every political decision. Take health insurance, for just one of the innumerable examples. More than eighty percent of our voters wanted the so-called Canadian health system of medical insuring, but the Clintons and other heavy-hitting policy makers never gave it so much as a look. Eighty to a hundred congressmen petitioned for its consideration, and the big money-aligned media gave that story a column inch for one day on page D-7.

This was no democracy, but an autocracy whose indentured citizenry is hypnotized with slogans and artful TV persuasions. How many million dollars does it take to elect a senator? Abe Lincoln, can you raise that much? And what will happen to your soul if you can and do?

Like Rome in Gospel days, we regulate by wealth and the sword and not by the vote or the popular will. We soothe our own people with pomp, sentiment, and ceremony, and then go out to militarily conquer and often occupy other nations, and in the process help keep our economy thriving, and our self-image narcissistically aflame with unrealistically inflated self-regard.

That we are roundly hated or ridiculed by the rest of the world's peoples worries us not a whit. When Reagan's murderous policies in Nicaragua were condemned by the World Court, we canceled our participation in the World Court, and our media gave out nary a sniff of reprobation for the latest lawless action.

Our own citizenry is quite deathly afraid of its own government, but afraid like a child living in a home headed by a bully alcoholic father, a child needing to comply and please in order to get by, and so afraid and brainwashed by the family denial system that he or she no longer knows for sure what he really sees, feels, or believes.

But there are symptoms that our sophisticated and well-financed denial system is breaking down, and that unpolitical, unprofitable murder is breaking out among the ranks of commoners, and against government orders.

Ancient Rome had its pressure valve of deadly games in the coliseums: the lions eating the Christians, and the gladiators hacking and stabbing each other until the plebeian spectators had their fill of watching Sunday's death and murder and pools of carmine blood resting atop the arena floor.

We have tried bloody football but, at last, football is no longer enough to sate us; it does not satisfy entirely. Outside our magnificent new stadiums, sudden military-style group murders of our own innocent civilians continue to occur in growing numbers at the hands of white Protestant males.

Perhaps it is time to try actual death in the coliseum again, but a modern version. Give black drug dealers a chance to get out of prison by fighting until one opponent dies in front of us. Feed imprisoned pacifist demonstrators to our native American cougars or groups of wolverines. Watch the number of senseless mass killings that has baffled our news anchors and pundits reduce measurably. When in Rome, do as Romans do.

BUT I WAS A boy in America before it turned into Rome, and I was living in a middle-class American neighborhood when middle class was actually rather poor by today's standards, although nobody thought so then. One car, if there was a car, one parent working. One bathroom in the house, and so on. This was before we got a swelled head and thought of ourselves as a world power; Ike was still overseas fighting the Nazis.

It was during these years that Burt Darrow died. Burt Darrow and his younger brother Carrow lived in our neighborhood along with a lot of other kids. Carrow was my age, about nine or ten, and Burt was light years older, perhaps seventeen, like a man to me, or at least a far superior being. And being seventeen or so would alone have been enough to give Burt Darrow celebrity in my eyes, but he was supernaturally nice to boot, and I'd never known anyone like him.

I can't remember seeing Burt when he wasn't smiling broadly and good-naturedly, or when he didn't have time to engage me in friendly conversation. Though I didn't realize it at the time, I loved Burt, and I'm sure Burt loved me, and probably everyone else he encountered.

Then I heard Burt had taken seriously ill and could no longer get out of bed. I remember visiting him once, just once in his bedroom, and sure enough he was neatly tucked under the covers of his bed with the light turning into soft gold as it came through the old window shades and we talked and he looked at me cheerfully and lovingly as he always did. And a short time after I heard he had died, very, very young.

This made no sense to me. I was stunned and empty-headed from the news. And in a way I still am; my heart still aches at the memory of it.

Descartes is famous for saying, "I think, therefore I am." Burt Darrow's proof of existence would probably read more like, "I love, therefore I want to be." But suddenly life-loving Burt Darrow stopped being, at least in the usual sense of the term, and I could never see why.

Which is why a lot of people have trouble believing in God. Like if there's a God, how could he let Burt Darrow die? How could God let Aunt Sophie die? How could God let all those Jews in the prison camps die?

Do you remember reading about Tom Grant, the businessman who chose a life of Franciscan voluntary poverty? Tom tells people he's on his eighth or ninth life; he's just not sure.

The first time Tom escaped death was on a whitewater river trip when he got catapulted out of a raft and swept down under the water and into a large hole among the rocks and held prisoner there, submerged by the powerful current. It was very quiet all around him as he tried to swim back up to the surface while the current held him suspended in watery space. Then he remembered last night's campfire when the guide talked about escaping just such a predicament by cutting off his life preserver and swimming downward until he came out the other end of the hole and up to the river surface. Only thing was Tom wasn't packing a knife, but he swam down anyway, against all natural instinct, life preserver and all, and in a few agonizingly long seconds bobbed gasping to the surface of the roiling river.

The second time was due to a pilot's error in a small corporate airplane. A simple mistake, not filling one of the gas tanks, and Tom and the pilot ran out of gas high in the sky, and before the emergency landing Tom was saying what he thought might be his final prayers.

The third time was ten years ago during a routine blood pressure check when a doctor discovered a small discolored mole on Tom and soon had taken from Tom's chest a piece of flesh the size of your hand. Tom had stage four melanoma and was given six months to live. Coincidentally, Tom's diocesan bishop had the same diagnosis and the same prognosis, but unlike Tom, died right on the schedule the doctors had predicted.

The fourth time was in 1992 when a heavy black BMW went out of control and slammed into Tom's carport at high speed just when Tom had stepped outside to view some red gladioli. The car smashed the support posts and the heavy carport roof came crashing down at Tom's feet. The shrapnel and debris cut into his lower body and he was in pain for weeks. A fifty-three-pound boulder went sailing between his legs and was later found in his living room. One of his sandals was discovered under the front bumper of the ruined car that had come within inches of killing him.

Then a week later some teenagers lost control of their car which came careening down the hill in the back of his home knocking down small trees and bushes and landing one foot from his driveway.

It was about then Tom and his wife decided to get out of town, sold their goods, and entered the Franciscan community.

In 1997, Tom had his first heart attack, and on the way to being driven to the hospital he stopped to use a service station restroom and passed out on the floor. The ambulance came for him and he woke up in intensive care. That might be his nearest near-death experience. He said it was a peaceful experience. He's still not sure if he was clinically dead at the time. We could call this number six.

A year ago he was diagnosed with colon cancer and they took out two feet of his colon, and all the lymph nodes and everything else remotely attached to his colon. The doctors didn't offer a life expectancy prediction, and Tom didn't ask.

Then just a few months ago, while he was carrying the Bible up to the altar during mass, he suffered what might have been his second heart attack—the pains, the sweating, the inability to breathe, but he did his duty, got seated, had a quick nitroglycerin tablet and, lo and behold, felt O.K. again.

Tom is a jolly man and people are often laughing around him. He's white-haired and white-bearded and looks something like Santa Claus, or an aging Friar Tuck, or a merciful and happy God the Father, the sort that would let you into Heaven if you really wanted to get in, no matter what you had done in the past. He has always encouraged me in my writing efforts, and when I read him the words that follow, all the way to the end of this section on murder, he broke down and wept, in something of the same way he had wept when his sudden conversion occurred more than fifteen years before.

He knew the words applied to him, as well as to me and you.

So eventually it does come around to yourself. How could God let you die? And since God alone has the power of life and death (if there is a God) then you know in some form or another God is going to kill (read murder) you. At worst, just like he killed Burt Darrow and Aunt Sophie, for no apparent reason.

God is the number one murderer, bar none. God, if there is a God, has been killing everything and everyone he breathed life into since life began, and foreseeably will go on killing in what almost looks like a compulsive fashion for as long as there is any life left in the physical universe. Maybe this constitutes part of our attraction to murder: that in some ways it seems God-like.

Anyway, you, my friend, are about to get killed, and when that end comes, all the time leading up to it will seem no greater than one wink of your eye. How do you feel about that? What are you going to do about that? If you happen to be a Benedictine monk your monastic rule will require you to remind yourself each morning that this could be the day that you die. And it could. The body being whisked away after the head-on colli-sion was inhabited by somebody who earlier that morning was trying to remember in which drawer or purse she'd put her airline tickets to Paris. And the proud father who tumbled head-first dead out of the grandstands with a busted blood vessel in his brain had just been crossing his fingers and praying his son would retire the side in that inning of Little League baseball. Death can and does come suddenly and without warning at times. Your life as you know it can get taken away, sometimes on the day you most wanted to hang on to it.

No wonder so many people are angry at God, some so angry they won't even acknowledge his existence.

SO THE PLOT THICKENS, and eventually you realize that the multiple murder mystery you are living in and trying to solve has you as its final victim. And that the murderer, if it's who you suspect it is, has worn any number of fantastic disguises in carrying out his past crimes: sometimes an abortion doctor, sometimes a prison guard, sometimes a psychotic killer, sometimes a surgeon on an off day, sometimes a deadly virus, sometimes the rock that tripped someone in an accidental fall, but behind it all, that most murder-ous genius, God. If there is a God.

Well, it is a murder mystery.

Murder because everyone is dying, and almost everyone against their will; and mystery because no one really knows for sure how they got here in the first place, and what they're doing here, and what, if anything, hap-pens afterwards.

Once in a great while, just a few times at most in my lifetime, I have seen out of the corner of my eye a sudden indirect glimpse of the gravity and size of the total amount of human suffering going on in this world at any one moment, and the sight has kept me reeling for at least a few days afterwards. Not all of us undergo sustained and great suffering during our earthly days, but plenty of us do, and if there is no recompense for it then the whole creation is nothing but an angry joke.

But just as all the random and confusing pieces fell into place when we first found out Nixon was lying about his role in Watergate, so all the anger, dread and compromise begin softening and sweetening when we grasp that the promise of the Gospels is true and that this life we are all waiting to die out of leads into the consuming love of God and the Heavenly life hereafter.

I AM WRITING THESE last words in the interest of truth while sitting on a humble couch in a humble home in rural Alabama. The home is in the black side of town, a town divided in two by the railroad tracks that run through it, and I'm on the poorer side. My godfather, Ernesto Cardenal, the great Nicaraguan poet and revolutionary who helped overthrow the U.S.-supported murderous tyrant Somoza, told me we all had to take sides, that we had to either take up residence with the oppressed group of humans on the planet, or live with the oppressing group, and I am slowly, slowly entering into understanding what he meant by those words.

If I want to drive to the white side of town, the side where most of the businesses are, the Walmarts, the supermarkets, and the smaller franchises like Burger King and Colonel Sanders, I had best drive by way of the main street that runs all the way through this small enclave of seven thousand souls. This street is named Martin Luther King Drive here on the black side of town, but when you drive over the railroad tracks it's named Medical Park Drive, in honor of the hospital that graces its route, the hospital that sent black African American Mark Parker off to his death on a slow mule cart about fifty years ago (legal murder through Jim Crow laws).

I'm sitting in the living room of Mark Parker's widow, my saintly mother-in-law, Mrs. Nellie Lee Parker, and Mrs. Parker is soundly sleeping now because it's nearing midnight. When she awakens she'll see Happy Birthday written over her fireplace in large shining letters, and there will be lots of colored balloons in the room, and after lunch a birthday cake with candles shaped like the number eighty-nine because Mother Parker will be a year short of ninety in the morning. People will be coming by and phoning from far away to celebrate her.

Mother Parker told me today she feels blessed that God has let her live so long. As always she spent a good deal of her time singing Baptist hymns around the house, taking every part in the choir including the solo parts and never missing a beat or a note. As always she spent a good deal of time laughing because life so delights her, and groaning because it also brings elements that elicit her sorrow.

She told me at some length about being present at the death of her grandfather. He and her grandmother had gotten just too old to look after one another, and although young Nellie Lee loved learning in the classroom, she asked her mother for permission to drop out of high school in the ninth grade so she could take care of these two old people, and she moved into their home which was about a day's journey away. When she was younger yet they had largely raised her because her mother had to be off working, and she loved these old folks as if they were mother and father.

One night about two o'clock in the morning fourteen-year-old Nellie was awakened by the sound of her grandmother going back and forth to and from the kitchen, the kitchen being in a small building outside the house, and connected by a short causeway. Young Nellie got out of bed and stood in the doorway of her grandparents' bedroom just as her grandmother came in with a large pot of steaming hot water.

Grandfather was in bed and praying joyfully to God. Nellie Lee remembers his last words: "I'm coming, Lord! I'm coming, Lord!" Then she remembers he fell silent and restful, and in a short while before the dawn he was gone from his body, and had died.

I don't think it could ever occur to Mother Parker now that she isn't soon to meet her maker, God, Jesus, and all the people she loved in this lifetime who are now on the other side, including her husband, Mark, who had to leave her a half-century ago, and her grandparents, who are even longer gone. And this belief agrees with her. It contributes to her great and remarkable, powerful but humble sense of well-being, just as it cheered the other saint I had the luck to meet over fifty years ago, Ma Watkins, in a small town named Huntington Beach, California.

Witty men have proved to their own satisfaction that Heaven cannot possibly exist. The poet Auden asks that we learn their logic, note their enormous simple grief, and let them teach us to doubt so we can then believe.

I cannot argue you into a belief in the Resurrection,
I cannot reason you into knowing you will rise again

with Jesus the son of God
Whose risen body contains the cosmos
that is now itself being crucified,
and with all nature, including yours:
is groaning towards the resurrection of everything:
every tin can and rusting tractor,
every reprobate and holy bishop,
every hanged felon, and every dainty nun,
all of us, all of us,
the long and the short and the tall.

Eye has not seen, nor has ear heard, what's in store for you after you're murdered at last. Your own risen body will be as different from the one you now inhabit as a stalk of wheat is from a grain of wheat; as different as an apple tree is from an apple seed; as different as a soaring colorful butterfly is from a grubby caterpillar.

Jesus, the first of the resurrected, was no Lazarus: Lazarus was a resuscitated man who was brought back to mortal life in his old mortal body. It was only a matter of time before Lazarus underwent his final mortal ending. But after Jesus died his immortal and resurrected body passed through walls and moved outside the dimensions of time and space as we know them. And he still does.

Try not to fight it. Think of it as foreplay. When you finally succumb you'll wonder why you put if off for so long. Let him kill you, and pray that he kills you softly.

Epilogue

Movies, not books, are today's popular art form, and I'm surprised at how often the critics miss the movie director's message and point of view entirely. In Spike Lee's *Do the Right Thing*, the drunken mayor who spends his time sitting on the steps watching the fighting between blacks and whites rather than joining with either side, and who also slowly and successfully woos the lovely lady upstairs, gets to speak the line, "Do the right thing," to Spike Lee as Spike rushes off to join in the race war. The drunken mayor *is* doing the right thing and embodies the movie's message: make love not war (interracially and every other way). The critics don't notice him and miss the movie's point.

In *Jungle Fever*, Spike Lee has black Lawrence Fishburne involved in a prolonged tragic and totally lustful affair with a white woman. In contrast, white John Turturro is involved in a growing and loving relationship with a young black woman. Spike Lee is again dramatizing how to get things right. Make love not lust. The critics miss the point again.

By the way the critics also never wrote about the drug industry being behind the frame-up in Harrison Ford's *The Fugitive*. The doctor Harrison played is trying to expose the lethality of a soon to be popular drug named "Provasic," and the drug manufacturers are out to kill him rather than lose their profits. They've already killed his wife and another doctor. Nary a mention of this by the professional film analysts, even though it provides the story's climactic scene.

And in that other, now antiquated art form, books, there is a long history of poets and novelists who wrote complaints about critics missing their work's central message, missing "the point."

Chaucer's extraordinary work of genius, *The Canterbury Tales*, is about Christian forgiveness, but I've never known a scholar to say so, perhaps in part because they don't bother to value, or perhaps even read, the only two prose tales (both on forgiveness) which are left out of most editions of the otherwise purely poetic story.

Since one of the two prose tales is told by the character of Chaucer himself, who plays the book's narrator, and the other by the Parson, whom Chaucer designates as the most virtuous person on the pilgrimage, you would think this enough in the way of clues for the learned and professional understanders, but no.

And finally, in the ultimate bestseller, the Bible, which is more than a book in much the same way that Man is more than an ape (yes, the Bible is a book. Yes, Man is an ape), the point is again Forgiveness.

Chaucer understood the Bible.

To help critics along then, let me be clear: the point of the book these words serve as epilogue to is the salvation of all humanity (and all the rest of the cosmic creation) in the sacrifice and resurrection of Jesus, that legendary Jew from Israel and all points.

May the grace of the Lord Jesus be with you all.

Bibliography

Bible.

Canterbury Tales by Geoffry Chaucer.

Chaucer's Bawdy by Thomas Wynne Ross.

Christ and the Universe: Teilhard de Chardin and the Cosmos by Robert Hale.

Consumer Reports, "High Anxiety," January 1993, pp.19-24.

Cosmic Canticle by Ernesto Cardenal.

Damien the Leper by John Farrow.

Death of the Messiah by Raymond Brown.

Distant Mirror by Barbara Tuchman.

Divine Comedy by Dante Alighieri.

Drinking the Mountain Stream by Milarepa.

A Marginal Jew: The Search for the Hiistorical Jesus by Rev. John P. Meier.

People of the Lie by M. Scott Peck.

Phenomenon of Man by Pierre Teilhard de Chardin.

Revelations of Divine Love by Julian of Norwich.

Scientific American, "Nutrients that Modify Brain Function," April 1982, pp.50-59, by Richard J. Wurtman.

Sexuality of Christ in Renaissance Art and in Modern Oblivion by Leo Steinberg.

Songs of Innocence and of Experience by William Blake.

Tao of Physics by Fritjov Capra.

Tao te Ching by Lao-tzu.

Theology Digest, "Dare we hope for the salvation of all? Origen, Gregory of Nyssa, Isaac of Nineveh," by Kalistos Ware: Volume 45, Number 4, Winter 1998, pp.302-317.

Thomas Merton's complete works.

Toxic Psychiatry by Peter Breggin.

Virginal Conception & Bodily Resurrection of Jesus by Raymond Brown.

CPSIA information can be obtained at www.ICGtesting.com
Printed in the USA
LVOW11s2003130716

496099LV00001B/77/P